Beechers, Stowes, and Yankee Strangers

The Florida History and Culture Series

University Press of Florida

Gainesville · Tallahassee · Tampa · Boca Raton · Pensacola · Orlando · Miami · Jacksonville

John T. Foster, Jr., and Sarah Whitmer Foster

BEECHERS, STOWES, AND YANKEE STRANGERS

The Transformation of Florida

Foreword by Raymond Arsenault and Gary R. Mormino

To Barbara

Sarah Whitmer Foster

John T Foster

Copyright 1999 by the Board of Regents of the State of Florida
Printed in the United States of America on acid-free paper
All rights reserved

05 04 03 02 01   6 5 4 3 2

Library of Congress Cataloging-in-Publication Data
Foster, John T., Jr.
Beechers, Stowes, and Yankee strangers: the transformation of Florida / John T.
Foster, Jr., and Sarah Whitmer Foster; foreword by Raymond Arsenault and
Gary R. Mormino.
p. cm. — (Florida history and culture series)
Includes bibliographical references and index.
ISBN 0-8130-1646-0 (acid-free paper)
1. Reconstruction—Florida. 2. Florida—History—1865–
3. Florida--Biography. I. Foster, Sarah Whitmer. II. Title.
III. Series.
F316 .F695   1999
975.9'061—dc21   98-49291

The University Press of Florida is the scholarly publishing agency for the State
University System of Florida, comprising Florida A & M University, Florida
Atlantic University, Florida International University, Florida State University,
University of Central Florida, University of Florida, University of North
Florida, University of South Florida, and University of West Florida.

University Press of Florida
15 Northwest 15th Street
Gainesville, FL 32611-2079
http://www.upf.com

To sources of love, energy, and faith in our lives:

Herbert B. Whitmer, Jr.

Louise C. Whitmer

Bruce Whitmer Foster

Jolene P. Foster

Roland S. Foster

Ann H. Foster

CONTENTS

FOREWORD

Beechers, Stowes, and Yankee Strangers: The Transformation of Florida is the eighth volume of a new series devoted to the study of Florida history and culture. During the past half-century, the burgeoning population and increased national and international visibility of Florida have sparked a great deal of popular interest in the state's past, present, and future. As the favorite destination of countless tourists and as the new home for millions of retirees and other migrants, modern Florida has become a demographic, political, and cultural bellwether. But, unfortunately, the quantity and quality of the literature on Florida's distinctive heritage and character has not kept pace with the Sunshine State's enhanced status. In an effort to remedy this situation—to provide an accessible and attractive format for the publication of Florida-related books—the University Press of Florida has established the Florida History and Culture series. As coeditors of the series, we are committed to the creation of an eclectic, carefully crafted set of books that will provide the field of Florida studies with a new focus and will encourage Florida researchers and writers to consider the broader implications and context of their work.

The series will include standard academic monographs, works of synthesis, memoirs, and anthologies. While it will feature books of historical interest, we encourage authors researching Florida's environment, politics, literature, and popular and material culture to submit their manuscripts for inclusion in the series. We want each book to retain a distinct "personality" and voice, but at the same time we hope to foster a sense of community and collaboration among Florida scholars.

In *Beechers, Stowes, and Yankee Strangers*, Professors John T. and Sarah Foster, colleagues in the Department of Sociology at Florida Agricultural and Mechanical University in Tallahassee, offer a sophisticated and provocative reinterpretation of Florida's Reconstruction era. For nearly a century Florida historians uniformly treated the Reconstruction experience as a misguided and tragic experiment in biracial democracy, dismissing any evidence to the contrary as Yankee-inspired propaganda. Only in the late 1960s, after the civil rights movement and the Sunbelt migration had opened the state to new ideas and new perspectives, did it become possible to challenge the politically and racially biased orthodoxies of neo-Confederate and white supremacist historiography. In a series of carefully researched monographs, Jerrell H. Shofner, Joe T. Richardson, and several other revisionist scholars began the process of painstakingly dismantling the mythic constructions that had obscured the complex realities of post–Civil War Florida. This process continues today, especially in an ongoing effort to reconsider the Reconstruction experiences of two important groups: African Americans and northern transplants. The latter group—traditionally derided and demonized as meddling and opportunistic Carpetbaggers—is the focus of the Fosters' efforts.

The "Yankee strangers" who dominate these pages were neither demons nor angels, but rather flesh-and-blood human beings who exhibited the entire range of human behavior and motivation. Sacrifice and opportunism, sympathy and condescension, tolerance and prejudice, courage and cowardice, conviction and doubt were all part of the Reconstruction story in Florida. The attempt to reconstruct the state involved a fascinating and somewhat improbable cast of characters, including the noted novelist Harriet Beecher Stowe, her eccentric brother Charles Beecher, the freedmen's dedicated schoolteacher Chloe Merrick Reed and her husband, Governor Harrison Reed, the crusading Methodist minister John Sanford Swaim, and a host of other Yankee schoolmarms, social reformers, aspiring politicians, and enterprising businessmen. Complicated and deepened by personal and familial entanglements, this vibrantly human network of Reconstructionists produced an ambitious reform program that held great promise for a state barely removed from the raw frontier.

Though politically truncated by the abrupt decline of the Florida Republican Party in the mid-1870s, the Reconstruction effort left an enduring cultural legacy that directly influenced Florida's development well into the twentieth century. As the Fosters demonstrate in their richly textured and moving narrative, the semi-actualized dreams of the Yankee strangers brought both progress and confusion to the Sunshine State. *Beechers, Stowes, and Yankee Strangers* is at once an inspiring saga and a book that promises to change our understanding of the most misunderstood era of Florida's past.

Raymond Arsenault and Gary R. Mormino
Series Editors

PREFACE

An Ebony Table and Yankee Strangers

One of us, John T. Foster, Jr., was raised near Jacksonville, Florida, where members of his family lived for several generations. His grandparents' house was exotic, far different from the simple dwellings of the postwar suburbs of the 1950s. Elegant English furniture stood beside paintings of Caribbean seacoasts. There were souvenirs of trips to Italy and India. On one table was a miniature marble fountain with tiny alabaster doves, each of the birds in a different pose, from landing with fluttering wings to perching peacefully. The fountain contrasted with a small ebony table. Less than two feet high, its exterior was carved with wooden leaves and vines. In the open spaces between the leaves, one could glimpse the interior, which held mementos of an earlier age. On top was a miniature silver tray with six matching cups and a teapot. Each gleamed in brightness, etched with diverse flowers.

As the years went by, John's grandparents sold the house, and most of the furniture and contents went to relatives or disappeared. Even so, the ebony table remained with his grandparents, and he once asked about its future. Since no one else had ever expressed any interest, John's grandmother bequeathed it to him. It would be a lasting link to her, to her exotic house, and to his life in her home when he was a child. When she gave it to him after his grandfather's death, he paid scant attention to it or its contents. In 1968 John graduated from college, sought his first job and hoped to find another draft deferment. Vaguely he remembered that the contents of the table had consisted of a photograph album of his grandfather's early voyages (years before he became a merchant marine officer), a small Italian pistol, field glasses, and a small pocket diary for the year 1866. The latter seemed fleetingly curious. It belonged, his grandmother merely said, "to uncle's grandfather."

When the diary came to our attention in the early 1980s, a brief glance proved it was more than just interesting. Its author was a minister with a multiracial ministry in Jacksonville. To our surprise, unlike many of the paternalists of the period, he apparently did not try to direct the lives of African Americans. Rather than making decisions for others, he consulted a local minister on the selection of the building site for a sanctuary; later he would write that he could not act because the church's trustees, most of whom were black, did not wish him to. Its author wrote newspaper articles. Why? Finding the newspaper and the articles only deepened the mystery. Rather than elaborating upon church life, they appeared to be publicity tracts created by a chamber of commerce. In 1865, the minister encouraged Yankees to invest in cotton plantations being abandoned by local planters. Within months he was praising opportunities in citrus groves and experimenting with growing vegetables in late winter.

The diary became a beguiling puzzle for both of us. It mentioned the incessant comings and goings of persons such as A. E. Kinne and Harrison Reed. At first only Reed seemed important because he became a governor of Florida. Also appearing in the diary was the name Chloe Merrick, unknown to us at first.

After years of pursuit, which took us through thousands of pages of unindexed newspapers, the diary turned out to be a golden thread leading us into the heart of the Reconstruction era and to Harriet Beecher Stowe and her brother, Charles Beecher. Chloe Merrick, herself a remarkable person, married Harrison Reed, and, inspired by her passion to transform education, her husband appointed Charles Beecher to his cabinet as state superintendent of public instruction. Our efforts to learn about Beecher in turn led to the discovery of forgotten publications by Stowe and to a new understanding of her activities in the South. The diary revealed threads of a complex tapestry—a different world, one of faith, vision, and imagination.

Corresponding with her friend Oliver Wendell Holmes, Harriet Beecher Stowe observed, "Dear Doctor, How time slips by! I remember when Sumner seemed to be a young man and now he has gone. [Salmon] Chase, whom I knew as a young man in society, has gone, and Stanton has gone and Seward has gone, and yet how lively the world races on."[1] And the world has raced on, knowing little of her presence in Florida or the contributions made by the Stowes and Beechers—Charles, James, and Eunice.

Lack of knowledge arises from scholars' failing to recognize participation of these visionaries within a community of like-minded, influential, and energetic reformers intent on transforming the state. Both Harriet Beecher Stowe and Charles Beecher joined a small group of "Yankee strangers," as those from the North were once called. Together they gave birth to modern Florida well before Henry Flagler came and built the Florida East Coast Railroad. By tracing the world of tourists, northern immigrants, and citrus groves to activists in the 1860s and 1870s, one can get a perspective different from that of most of the historical literature.

Generally historians have stressed railroad builders in the 1880s and 1890s, with only a handful of scholars looking to earlier decades. In 1938 one of these scholars, state librarian William T. Cash, wrote, "During the Reconstruction there were many northern immigrants, and it was then that the development of Central and South Florida really began."[2] In the next sentence Cash turns to the Beechers and the Stowes: "For several years Mrs. Harriet Beecher Stowe, author of *Uncle Tom's Cabin*, lived in Florida and here wrote a book of impressions. Her brother, Charles Beecher, moved to Newport in Wakulla County soon after the close of the Civil War and was living quietly at this place when he was appointed State Superintendent of Public Instruction."[3]

When Junius E. Dovell, a professor at the University of Florida, sought the origins of citrus production, "the greatest agricultural boom of post-bellum Florida," he reached a similar conclusion: "The 'orange fever' was probably encouraged by the reports of Mrs. H. B. Stowe's small grove which told of fabulous returns from those trees and other small groves scattered about the state."[4] For evidence Dovell cites an account of the period: "A man can enter one hundred and sixty acres of first class land at a cost of fifteen dollars for fees. A temporary house of pine logs will be sufficiently comfortable for the climate. If able-bodied, with his own labor he can clear and plant ten acres in orange trees the first year, and thence on, every year, add ten acres to his grove. In ten years the first ten acres ought to yield $1,000 dollars an acre. In eleven years the first will yield, probably $1,500 an acre, and the second ten, $1,000—an income of $25,000. In sixteen years, at this rate, he will have 160 acres of solid grove, and the income of a [prince]."[5]

In more recent times Thomas Graham of St. Augustine looked to the decade before Flagler's residence in the Ancient City and gave credit to Stowe: "Harriet Beecher Stowe penned marvelous stories to magazine readers in the North, describing the magic by which winter could be turned into spring simply by stepping aboard an express train to the Land of Flowers." As a result, "thousands of perfectly healthy, mostly wealthy people were taking Mrs. Stowe's advice and visiting the state for the sheer pleasure of it."[6]

The following account acknowledges Harriet Beecher Stowe's contributions as well as those of other visionary Yankees. Having lived with this remarkable story for many years, we use a term that predates a common one. This story is about Yankees in the South in the Civil War and Reconstruction. Many writers refer to these people as "carpetbaggers." Such a label, if applied to the persons in this book, would be the epitome of injustice. We use the expression "Yankee strangers" for Northerners who took up residence in the South between 1862 and 1877.

We are profoundly indebted to Samuel Proctor and Canter Brown, Jr. As the editor of the *Florida Historical Quarterly*, Dr. Proctor responded to numerous drafts of our papers for more than a decade. He invariably asked difficult questions and offered suggestions that dramatically improved our efforts. This book rests upon a foundation that reflects his thoughtful encouragement. Canter Brown's involvement has also been crucial. He shared knowledge, sources, and drafts of his forthcoming books. We are also indebted to him for ideas about the structure of this work and for the encouragement to persevere in writing. Without Canter's collegiality this book would not exist.

A National Endowment for the Humanities summer seminar (1984) gave us an invaluable framework for comparing early educational developments in Florida to those in other places in the South. The seminar rested upon the outstanding scholarship of Robert F. Engs, professor of American history at the University of Pennsylvania.

We also wish to acknowledge the loving and thoughtful interest of Bruce Robertson, Edna Danielson, Charlotte Bostwick, Emmit Hunt, Ann Riccardi, Jonathan Larson, and Mary Kay Larson. Their kindness has been a source of joy in a sometimes grueling process. Our thanks should also go to a number of professionals for their assistance and encouragement: Mark I. Greenberg, Museum of the Southern Jewish Experience; David J. Coles, Florida State Archives; Cynthia C. Wise, Florida Collection, State Library of Florida; Joan Morris and Jody Norman, Florida Photographic Collection, Florida State Archives; Judy Haven, Onondaga Historical Association, Syracuse; and Patsy Verreault, Union Theological Seminary Library. Roxane Fletcher deserves special thanks for being a remarkable line editor.

PROTECT THE BIRDS

The Legislature of Florida meets in January, and cannot *The Semi-Tropical* rouse some one to present before them the claims of the birds of Florida to protection.

Florida has been considered in all respects as a prey and a spoil to all comers. Its splendid flowers and trees, its rare and curious animals have been looked upon as made and created only to please the fancy of tourists—to be used and abused as the whims of the hour might dictate. Thousands of idle loungers pour down here every year, people without a home or landed interest in the State, and whose only object seems to be to amuse themselves while in it without the least consideration of future results to the country.

The decks of boats are crowded with men, whose only feeling amid our magnificent forests, seems to be a wild desire to shoot something, and who fire at every living thing on shore, careless of maiming, wounding or killing the living creatures which they see, full of life and enjoyment. Were they hunters expecting profit of any kind from the game, there might be apology and defence for this course. But to shoot for the mere love of killing is perfect barbarism, unworthy of any civilized man, and, unless some protection shall be extended over the animal creation, there is danger that there may be a war of extermination waged on our forests.

This essay was originally published in the January 1877 issue of *The Semi-Tropical*, and appears here for the first time since its original publication. Stowe's punctuation and spelling have been retained.

Besides the guns of hunters, the birds of Florida are exposed to the incursions of bird trappers, who come regularly every year and trap and carry off by thousands and tens of thousands the bright children of our forests. These birds die by hundreds in the passage to New York and Europe. It is a perfect slave trade over again, and it is slowly and surely robbing our beautiful State of one of its chief attractions.

The number of red birds, mocking birds, and nonpareils has very sensibly diminished in Duval county within the last five years. That which used to be a constant source of pleasure and delight in their song and plumage is becoming a rarity, and if things go on many years more as they have done, it will cease altogether.

There may be those who will have little care for this. There are those who care nothing for beauty or for song—but who are dead set, only and fully on something to eat. They accuse the birds of stealing their peas and grapes, and declare that they would be glad to see them exterminated.

Have they ever reflected, what else birds eat beside peas and grapes? Have they reflected that they are all the while searching the ground for insects—for the eggs and larvae of what will become destructive to vegetation? The bird eats a pea, to be sure, for his salad, but he takes a dozen cut-worms for his meat. Guided by unerring instinct they pick the corn worm from its green shell—they find the burrows and holes where the eggs of destructive insects are hid and pick them out.

Now, in the cold Northern States where the winter freezes the noxious insects and keeps down their increase, still the value of birds as guardians against their ravages is so well known, that protective laws exist in most of the Northern States, to prevent the reckless destruction of the feathered tribes.

How much more do we need bird help in the hot, teeming soil of Florida, where the ground never freezes and where insect life swarms in every direction. We had better pay the taxes of a few peas and grapes and have the birds for under gardeners, than to suffer as some of the Western States are now suffering by losing crop after crop through grasshoppers.

An army of mocking birds would soon make an end of grasshoppers. These light guerrilla warriors, feathered and mailed, are God's own police, meant to search out and keep down the noxious abundance of animal life, where the dull eye of man cannot see and the slow foot of man cannot tread. Those bright, quick eyes and buoyant wings, go up and down searching, picking, devouring.

Florida is now setting out thousands of orange groves, and, if nothing happens, may have a harvest golden as the Hesperides. But what if the orange insect comes down upon us as the grasshoppers have in the West? Is it not safer to protect the birds?

Who, now, will appear for the birds? Who will get a protection law passed that will secure to us the song, the beauty and the usefulness of these charming fellow citizens of our lovely Florida?

Harriet Beecher Stowe
Mandarin, Fla., Dec. 1876

Harriet Beecher Stowe
and Reform in the South

"This morning being Sunday, he called, Beecher!
Beecher! Very Volubly. He evidently is a progressive bird and
. . . may yet express himself on some of the questions of the day."

Harriet Beecher Stowe, speaking of her pet bird,
Phoebus, a fellow resident in her Florida home[1]

At the heart of Harriet Beecher Stowe's thoughts about living in the South lay a desire to participate in its transformation into a progressive place. African Americans had been freed by the Civil War, and she worried about their well-being. Corrupt politicians seemed to her ready to exploit them. After Stowe came to Florida in 1867, she allied herself with a small group of Yankees equally bent on change. The remarkable story of this group and their relationship with the Beechers and the Stowes is an adventure in the unexpected. A part of the South became forever different.

Harriet Beecher Stowe's interest in social reform had complex roots. While a teenager, she was inclined toward the ministry. Denied the pulpit because of her gender, she instead pursued her objectives through writing. In 1829 she wrote, "I was made for a preacher—indeed in a certain sense it is as much my vocation to preach on paper as it is that of my brothers to preach via voice."[2]

As years passed, she came under the spell of perfectionism. The notion that groups and individuals could significantly improve themselves was widespread among intellectuals in the 1840s, and many utopian communities sprang up in the United States. In the same period, efforts to improve herself frustrated her. Burdens arising from the births of sickly children and the difficulties of managing a household overwhelmed Stowe. Pain, frustration, and grief led to a conversion experience. In her deepest despair she gave herself to a bleeding savior. By realizing God's grace, she no longer sought self-perfection. Yet the idea of improving "society" remained. After a son died of cholera in 1849, she channeled her desire for social change and her anguish over his death into writing *Uncle Tom's Cabin.*[3]

Her passion for changing society was wedded to a concern for the common person. Agreeing with Martin Luther, she observed, "I preach not for learned men and magistrates."[4] Seeking a wider audience, she continued to pursue a form of personal ministry. The needs of children, women, and the least of society were vital to her. Answers to many of their problems were to be found in faith and in the New England of her youth. As the United States became ever more captured by the industrial revolution, Stowe returned in thought and novels to the village life of the past. The common school, education, and participation in democracy offered answers for oppressed factory workers and for immigrants from abroad. New England offered a blueprint for America.[5]

The portion of the South to which Stowe came in the years after the Civil War remained largely uninhabited. With fewer than 200,000 residents, according to the 1870 census, Florida was both the least populated and the poorest southern state. A tourist trade existed, but it was small and relatively young. In 1870 14,000 tourists visited the area. By the middle of the decade, this number had grown to 50,000. Jacksonville by then had become the "most frequented resort, and the entrance gate to over two-thirds of the travel of the State." Before the Civil War, the town could boast only a few hotels. The Buffington had almost 100 rooms, and the Judson House had 110. Fire destroyed the former in 1859, and the latter was burned by a mob on March 11, 1862. The lack of earlier development led the southern poet Sidney Lanier to describe Jacksonville in 1876 as only recently joining the nineteenth century: "Previous to the war between the states it was a comparatively insignificant town. In 1866, I was informed that a careful census made under the auspices of the freedmen's bureau revealed but about 1,700 inhabitants in it, a majority of whom are said to have been Negroes drawing their main subsistence from the charity of the nation. The resident population is now between twelve and fourteen thousand and this number is largely increased during the winter."[6]

Tourism during the post–Civil War period usually centered on the St. Johns River and nearby attractions. Visitors enjoyed excursions on the river and, of course, often journeyed on to St. Augustine. Travel offered challenges unknown today. One visitor going to St. Augustine described the railroad "as the very worst in the world." To this comment he added, "It was not a special honor for me to ride on the water tank with a pine knot for a footstool, for it was shared with other passengers. The fact is there are but two passenger cars on the road, and they had been monopolized by a group from Jacksonville. There was nothing left for us but an old locomotive compounded out of a pumping engine, a dirt excavator and the safety valve of a ferry boat, and tender which held two 10-gallon water tanks and a wood pile."[7] The train moved slowly, especially through swamps. Rather than building a bridge, the railroad company had created a causeway out of logs. To these were affixed the "supports for the rails." The visitor observed, "It is not a cheerful operation to go over a swamp a mile or two long filled with decaying and rotten pine logs." Yet many of the riders were in good cheer. At one of the slowest points, the traveler noted, "The engine slowed to about a mile in five hours; the bridge cracked and the locomotive groaned."[8]

Similar experiences with steamboats kept even some determined tourists away from more remote locations, such as Silver Springs. Harriet Beecher Stowe turned down a trip because of the appalling appearance of the vessel *Ocklawaha*. "We had always dreaded the boat as the abatement of pleasure," she recorded. Without glass windows, it resembled a "coffin in the twilight."[9]

At the beginning of her southern activities, Stowe enlisted the involvement of her brother, Charles Beecher. Talented as well as knowledgeable about the South, he had graduated from college at the age of nineteen. He had been forced to study for the ministry. In a period of rebellion, he fled to New Orleans, where he witnessed the lavish lifestyle of planters and the degrading abuse of slaves. On a trip to St. Louis, he met the real-life prototype of Simon Legree, a Yankee whose words Charles recorded: "I never see the n—— I couldn't bring down with one crack of the fist." To this statement the overseer added a horrifying claim: "When one's dead, I buy another. It becomes cheaper and easier, every way."[10] In writing her famous novel, Harriet Beecher Stowe needed details about life in the South. Her own experiences in the region were very limited, so she turned to her brother for factual content.[11] Charles responded with notes and personal assistance. Years later he helped her again by accompanying her on her journey to Jacksonville in 1867.

After Harriet Beecher Stowe and Charles Beecher came to Florida, they joined a group of like-minded activists. Many of the members of this group had arrived during the Civil War at Fernandina, a small but strategic port northeast of Jacksonville. Among these newcomers, or Yankee strangers, were an accomplished educator and administrator, a forty-nine-year-old newspaper man who desperately wanted to get into politics, and a prominent minister exiled to the South because of poor health. The coming chapters reveal the complex paths by which their lives intertwined and how the Beechers and Stowes joined them. Still other actors surrounded this group. They included a future high school principal, an army officer who would be called the "Prince of Carpetbaggers," and the would-be politician's multimillionaire sister. An account of these reformers in Florida is essential to understanding the lives of the Beechers and Stowes, for together they participated in a common agenda—the deliberate transformation of a state and of a people.

2

Civil War Fernandina

Among the first reformers to come to Florida from the North during the Civil War was Chloe Merrick. Less than ten years after her arrival, her influence helped bring Charles Beecher into the state's cabinet in 1871. Merrick's earlier experiences in Florida strengthened her determination. Long after most Yankee teachers returned home, she remained, true to her abolitionist roots, committed to the advancement of blacks.

Talented and persuasive, Chloe Merrick was born near Syracuse, New York, in 1832. She was the youngest member of the Merrick clan, known for ruggedness in body and independence of mind. Her mother died when she was a small child, and so she was raised by her father, Sylvanus, and by her two brothers, Montgomery and Charles, who were twenty and seventeen years older. Her sister, Emma, three years older than she, also was to influence her as a role model. About 1837 the family moved into Syracuse, prospering in an economy based upon the Erie Canal. Montgomery chose a career as a brick mason and contractor; Charles became a brick maker; and Emma, a teacher.[1]

As the Erie Canal brought commerce, it also served as a conduit for news and controversial ideas. Abolitionism was spreading in New England and the Midwest in the early 1840s, and the movement soon inspired the Merricks. At the time some Methodists were using John Wesley's rejection of slavery to confront the national denomination on its policy. In 1843 nine men, including Montgomery and Charles, forcefully raised the contradiction between the national church policy and that of its founder, Wesley. When they failed to influence the local Methodist congregation, they purchased a lot next door and organized a chapel affiliated with the Wesleyan Connection of America—a group whose creed included "no slaves" and "no rum."[2]

The Merricks' decision to join this denomination had unexpected consequences. On July 19, 1848, backers held the famous women's rights convention in a Wesleyan Connection church in nearby Seneca Falls. A denomination espousing freedom for African Americans provided a ready venue for those seeking freedom for women. A similar pattern followed in Syracuse. In 1852 Susan B. Anthony spoke in the Merrick home church, demanding "for her sex all of the rights enjoyed by men even to the ballot box."[3] Soon afterwards the Merricks' pastor, Luther Lee, published a sermon based upon Galatians 3:28: "There is neither male nor female; for ye are all one in Christ Jesus." From this starting point, he went on to note carefully examples of women who had served as Old Testament prophets and judges. Citing such evidence, he concluded that women had a "God given right to preach," and then he ordained Antoinette Brown as a minister.[4] Historians have described her as being the first woman in the United States to receive such authority.[5] As a member of the Wesleyan Connection, Chloe heard in the family church antislavery speeches and calls for women's equality. Young and impressionable, she was not afraid to translate ideas into action.

Mentored by her sister, Emma Merrick Kinne, and brother-in-law, Ansel E. Kinne, she embarked on a career as a teacher. As a teenager she lived in the household of the Kinnes, both of whom were educators. Ansel's students remembered him as different from other teachers, concerned with issues of social justice. According to a local historian, he took "seriously the biblical admonition to be concerned about one's neighbors whether they were African-Americans, women, or wayward youth. His sympathy for others made him popular with students, many of whom still praised him in the 1920s, decades after his death."[6] The Kinnes shared their knowledge of pedagogy, literature, and history with Chloe. This she added to what she learned in public lectures, attending speeches by Horace Mann, William Garrison, Frederick Douglass, and Gerrit Smith, with whom she later corresponded. Particularly important was the influence of the Reverend Samuel J. May, an uncle of Louisa May

Alcott. May not only championed abolitionism, but he also preached women's rights and a ban on capital punishment.[7] By listening to many of the leading intellectuals of the period, Merrick gained an education very different from that available to most young women of the period.

While many of the speeches attended by Merrick were informative, one was prophetic. Speaking from a balcony, on May 26, 1851, Daniel Webster chastised local abolitionists, and added a belief that enraged Wesleyans. The Fugitive Slave Law passed by Congress would be enforced in "spirit and in letter" in Syracuse even during "the next Antislavery Convention."[8] His prophecy came true in early October, when marshals arrested a runaway slave, Jerry Henry. Syracuse overflowed with people as the Liberty Party convened its meeting. The shocking news of Henry's arrest spread "like wildfire," and abolitionists descended upon the office where he was being held. Within minutes Henry plunged into the sympathetic crowd and fled. The onlookers temporarily blocked the police and Sylvanus Merrick "slammed the door and held it fast."[9] Unfortunately this effort failed when the marshals found Jerry Henry and in a struggle tore off half of his clothing. Thrown on the back of a dray, Henry was carried through the streets pleading, "For God's sake, kill me, don't send me back."[10] His despair spurred new action. In the evening the Merricks, Samuel J. May, and numerous others returned to the jail. "They smashed windows, chopped up casings, and battered down the jail door," one account detailed. Although marshals fired into the crowd, its members persevered and liberated Henry.[11]

Chloe's subsequent behavior suggests that this event taught her a number of lessons, the most salient being that the success of a cause required action that entailed personal risk. Authorities indicted both Montgomery and Sylvanus for their roles, and Merrick's father felt the need to seek refuge in Illinois "until the excitement blew over."[12] Additionally, the young woman could see that part of the success of the strategy came from careful planning. Rather than being just a mean-spirited mob, the abolitionists who attacked the jail scrupulously avoided harming the marshals. By only scaring the officers into flight, they achieved their goal and minimized the legal action that could be brought against them. In the end, abolitionists defied the Fugitive Slave Law in a manner that left them unpunished, thus undermining its enforcement.[13]

While Chloe may have participated in this victory, as women helped liberate Henry, her primary contribution was yet to come. Clearly, her family willingly translated ideas and ideology into action. In the meantime she taught in local schools and continued her professional relationship with Emma and Ansel. When Ansel served as the principal of an elementary school in the early 1860s, biographers noted that Merrick worked as one of his teachers. Later, even after Merrick came to Florida, their ties remained close.

With the Civil War's onset, events occurred that led Merrick on the path to affecting the course of Florida's future. When the Union army seized South Carolina's Sea Islands, it gave United States authorities control of fertile lands. As Federal forces extended their gains down the coast into northeast Florida, military commanders faced the increasingly enormous task of fighting hunger, malnutrition, and disease. The planters had abandoned their farms, taking with them clothing and medicine, and Federal soldiers, reportedly, consumed "all" of the "poultry, pigs and other eatables."[14] Thousands of African Americans in Federal territory achieved freedom but became destitute. The subsequent burdens on the military led to General Order No. 9 on February 6, 1862, calling for the "immediate action" of a "philanthropic people."[15] The army wanted to "relieve" itself of caring for former slaves and sought the assistance of teachers who would address basic needs.

This event led to the formation of freedmen's aid societies and to an organizational meeting on February 20, 1862. From it emerged an organization known as the National Freedmen's Relief Association (NFRA) and a series of guidelines. The freedmen, the NFRA proposed, were to "earn their livelihood" and be paid wages in the same manner as other citizens. Until this became possible, "they would be aided with food, clothing, and shelter" under the direction of "well-organized superintendents."[16] Duties would be given to teachers, who were expected to establish schools and churches. The teachers, in turn, were to encourage work rather than idleness, and the freedmen were expected to raise garden crops to feed their families.

Abolitionists in Syracuse were, as one might expect, sympathetic to the army's plan and to the NFRA guidelines. In the fall of 1862, Samuel May organized a local branch and secured enough funding to provide several teachers for Fernandina, Florida. Chloe Merrick, along with her friend Cornelia Smith, volunteered for service. By early November, a newspaper reported, "these heroic ladies [had] packed their wardrobes and quietly left for Port Royal, South Carolina."[17] On their journey south, the young women stayed several weeks near Hilton Head, exchanging information with teachers who had arrived earlier. From them they heard positive reports: African Americans were capable learners, and in spite of the many hardships, conditions were improving. During a visit to a school near Beaufort, Merrick met Charlotte Forten, one of the African American teachers serving in the Sea Islands. Forten soon noted to the *Boston Liberator* that Chloe "looked like an earnest worker."[18]

Merrick's Florida service quickly gathered steam. When she and Smith arrived in Fernandina, they found two small communities near a fort at the north end of Amelia Island. Most of the white southerners had fled months earlier, leaving 1,100 slaves. Of the black population, 200 men had enlisted in the Federal army. This left their families to be provided for, some 250 women and 416 children. The remainder of the black population either worked at the fort, fished, or suffered from physical disabilities. Besides African Americans and soldiers, several hundred civilians also lived on the island. This group was composed of Unionists, businessmen who rejected the Confederacy, and several Federal agents. Merrick and Smith discovered that a school was operating out of an abandoned Episcopal church. In a period of five months, it had had three teachers: a white soldier who was reassigned to active duty, an African American teacher, and an apathetic white Presbyterian minister. In spite of the turmoil, Chloe found that "seventy or eighty pupils [of all ages] had learned the alphabet and some were able to read quite understandingly."[19] On December 4 Chloe Merrick and Cornelia Smith began a routine they followed until school closed for the summer. In the morning both women taught for four hours, and in the afternoons they visited the homes of students. The latter proved to be very valuable since it enhanced parental support and provided the teachers themselves with a wealth of useful knowledge. They heard firsthand accounts of the tragedies of slavery and found a "spirit of determination and cooperation": "While many are destitute, they cling to each other by bonds of heart-sympathy, making the worst ills endurable."[20] The home visits also made them aware of local needs. "In calling among the people," Merrick recorded, "we find many suffering from colds, rheumatism and fevers," which resulted from the periodic cold weather and the lack of adequate clothing. The plight of shivering children led the teachers to exhaust their supply of donated clothing and to appeal for more. "Please send us," Merrick wrote, "articles that can be made useful."[21]

By March the number of students had climbed from 150 to 330. Such growth required the teachers to form a second school and to divide the student population into classes. Merrick took 130 of the more advanced students, ones who could "read well in the Bible reader" and those who could understand "easy sentences." The remainder, beginners who were learning their letters, joined Cornelia Smith in basic classes. In four months the students showed marked progress; Merrick noted that African American "children were capable of improvement equally with white children."[22]

The school year ended in May 1863, with a graduation ceremony. The African American community attended this event, along with officers from the fort and a number of government officials. Two men of particular significance for Florida's future watched—Federal Tax Commissioner Harrison Reed and Colonel Milton S. Littlefield. At the time, Harrison Reed was a forty-nine-year-old widower, much older than either Merrick or the officer. His physical appearance was unprepossessing; a rival tax commissioner described him as "an old granny."[23] Reed nonetheless had some appealing characteristics. As the founding editor of the *Milwaukee Sentinel*, he enjoyed a keen interest in literary affairs. To his ability to converse on current literature, Reed added talent and a very determined character. Like Merrick, he tenaciously pursued his aims.

Given her talent and accomplishments and her ability at persuasion, he was more than willing to assist her in her causes.

Even so, the two of them differed markedly in some ways. Reed, by temperament and politics, was far more conservative. His appointment in Florida had resulted from the influence of his sister's husband, Alexander Mitchell. Mitchell, an ally of Andrew Johnson, rejoined the Democrat party after the war. Perhaps even more important, Reed deeply admired his very successful brother-in-law's wealth. Mitchell had gained control of a bankrupt railroad and turned it into an empire worth millions. Reed was impressed by the Mitchells' estates, their private railcars, and their trips to Europe.[24]

Colonel Littlefield, on the other hand, was young, attractive, and ambitious, or even "magnetic." He had spent time as a child near Syracuse, and Merrick gave his troops a flag "blazoning the word 'Liberty'."[25] Littlefield invited Chloe on a picnic expedition to the ruins of a plantation. Needing a respite from her service work, she accepted his offer. As one historian describes it, "The ruined gardens were still magnificent. Bamboo, banana, fig and pomegranate grew wild around them. And behind the house, in which Union soldiers had scribbled inscriptions on the walls, a road ran for miles through a cool forest of moss-draped live oak."[26] Charlotte Forten wrote of such a place: "The air was soft, Italian."[27] While Littlefield evidenced a flair for romance and pretty girls, Merrick was both older and wiser than many. She found him charming yet short on substance. As Merrick reflected later, "I learned in the beginning not to compromise with those whose true interest in the cause is not fully known."

Chloe Merrick could have chosen between the "tall, dark haired" Littlefield who had "genial laughing eyes" or the small, "slightly built" Reed. Instead she was content to pursue her service goals, reflecting what was to be a lifelong concern for the plight of children. A newspaper of the time reported, "During her travels around Amelia Island," Merrick discovered a number of "utterly destitute, parentless, orphans of both races." She found three white children suffering from smallpox in a "jail-like place where they spent the winter."[28] As she informed the people of

Syracuse, "More destitution this side of nakedness and starvation one could not find."[29] The situation with African Americans was equally depressing. One black child had been held in servitude by an elderly freedwoman who looked upon orphans as having a market value. Chloe believed that the woman had been reduced to the same spiritual level as her former master.

The presence of orphans and abused children strongly suggested a need for an orphanage, so Merrick began organizing one. She shared her intentions with Harrison Reed, and he helped her purchase a large house at a tax sale. Its owner, Confederate general Joseph Finegan, was away fighting, and his property taxes had not been paid. In the same period, the summer of 1863, Merrick turned to military authorities, seeking their support and financial backing. The regional commander, General Rufus Saxton, responded to Chloe's personal request by providing three hundred dollars in cash, "sixty pairs of shoes, thirty blankets and clothing," as well as "axes, rakes, hoes, hatchets, saws, hammers, and other useful articles."[30]

While this response encouraged Merrick, additional funding was needed and she began a public campaign to obtain it. Before returning to Syracuse, she sent letters to its newspapers. To avoid seeming "too conspicuous before the public," behavior viewed as inappropriate for women at the time, the requests for financial aid came from both Reed and Samuel May. In describing the project, Reed noted that "Miss Merrick of your city first suggested the idea." Then he expressed his adamant confidence in her by adding, "her executive and administrative ability" will "guarantee its success."[31]

Merrick's mission thrust her into public life. Once in New York, she obtained the NFRA's endorsement and gave a number of public presentations. A highlight of the visit involved a dinner excursion for 300 people to Fulton, New York. As diners feasted under a large tent, they listened while Chloe and host Ansel Kinne described "the dire needs of Florida's blacks and orphans."[32] A local newspaper reported, "Miss Merrick's remarks were of an interesting character, giving an account of her labors among the refugees in Florida."[33] The Fulton trip also served as a public celebration recognizing Chloe Merrick's success as an educator. For years the anniversary of Jerry Henry's rescue had brought attention to the Merrick men. Now her time had come.

In her newfound public role, Chloe ardently pursued her vision. She involved others, seeking financial and personal support to guarantee the success of her work. Besides helping to recruit new teachers, she wanted to involve the Kinnes in her southern projects. She envisioned Emma as a supervisor in the orphanage and Ansel as a superintendent in the freedmen's schools. To encourage them, Merrick shared many details about living conditions and the additional victories that could be had for the cause of emancipation. As active Wesleyan Methodists, a group committed to ending slavery, the Kinnes responded enthusiastically. In December 1863, Ansel resigned from the public school system and made arrangements for his relocation to Fernandina. Emma Merrick Kinne made plans to come a year later so that she could bring their four children.[34]

The success of her efforts gave Merrick both financial and familial reinforcements and new energy. In October 1863 she returned to Fernandina to prepare the Finegan house for its new role. A large three-story structure measuring sixty feet by sixty feet, the house provided desperately needed space. Working at great speed, Merrick opened the orphanage early in 1864. The refuge held eighteen youthful residents by the end of the year and twenty-six children by February 1865. Within a year and a half, fifty children were in her care. The growing numbers and commensurate responsibilities brought significant problems. On occasions military authorities suspended rations for the destitute, cutting off a major source of food commodities for the children. Merrick's foresight had led her to provide her flock a backup by planting gardens. In 1866 she noted, "We have about twenty bushels of corn left which was raised on the place and forty dollars to go on with."[35]

As the population of the orphanage grew, Merrick managed through ingenuity to maintain the high quality of care. Numerous references—appearing in publications such as the *National Freedman*, where Merrick was listed as a teacher along with Sojourner Truth and Charlotte Forten, and in letters, diaries, and reminiscences of others—document the work of the orphanage. When Esther Hill Hawks, a medical doctor, visited in 1864, she found the children "neatly dressed and contented."[36] Praise also came from one man who "found the boys and girls in excellent condition. A more healthy and happy lot of children I have rarely seen."[37]

While the combination of planning and effort brought visible rewards, the pioneer environment brought personal risks. Sarah Slocum, a colleague from Syracuse who taught in Fernandina, died in the fall of 1864 and Emma Kinne became gravely ill in 1865. Chloe's own difficult bout with fever occurred a year later. Life near a military garrison provided other sorrows. Keen to recognize the problems of women, Merrick wrote about exploitation that arose from the presence of Federal troops. Soldiers seduced young black women and abandoned them after they became pregnant. Chloe reported, "Sarah, a young ebony girl, formerly a pupil in our schools, but now the mother of an infant comes to us for aid." Such cases stirred Merrick to feelings of rage, pity, and frustration. "We cry out from the depths of our soul, God," she exclaimed, "what lessons art thou teaching the nation in this scourge thou art permitting thus to visit this oppressed people?"[38]

While Merrick developed the orphanage, Harrison Reed struggled in his political arena, mostly with problems relating to the tax commission on which he served. Another tax commissioner, Lyman D. Stickney, owed his appointment, unlike Reed's, to Salmon P. Chase, Abraham Lincoln's able and ambitious secretary of the treasury. Chase had two abiding interests: furthering the cause of racial equality and advancing his own political career.[39] In pursuing these goals, he was "no unprincipled politician who would make appointments for only personal gain."[40] Stickney, on the other hand, fed the secretary's ambitions but lacked the honesty that Chase's agents normally possessed.

With warring personal ambitions and different political loyalties, Stickney and Reed soon engaged in bitter conflict. The results clouded the legality of tax sales and led to Reed's forced resignation from the panel late in 1863. Out of office, he set out to get another federal position. "I have embarked in schemes for the benefit of the freedmen and I want to live in Florida to assist in bringing it in as a free state," he informed others.[41] In order to be close to Chloe and supportive of her efforts, Reed used the help of Wisconsin contacts to finagle an appointment as President Andrew Johnson's chief postal agent for Florida, a position he finally obtained in 1865.

By the time Ansel Kinne arrived in Fernandina in February 1864, Chase's supporters had, of course, prevailed. While Kinne was not impressed with Stickney, he shared the secretary's views on emancipation. Chase had gained renown by defending African Americans legally and by attacking commonly held views of the Constitution. Chase observed that the Constitution's authors addressed slavery without defending it. By looking at the intentions of early political leaders, he found avenues for interpretation—ones helpful to African Americans. Chase held power in the Republican party, and, as the Civil War dragged on without resolution, frustrations with Lincoln grew. For a period before the 1864 political campaign and General William Tecumseh Sherman's victories, attention focused upon Chase as a potential alternative to Lincoln. Although this opportunity evaporated, his desire to be president remained.

As Lincoln recovered politically, an exhausted and unhappy Chase resigned from the Treasury in 1864—a decision rapidly followed by a new opportunity. The Chief Justice of the Supreme Court, Roger B. Taney, died in the fall of 1864, and Lincoln nominated Chase as his successor. The Senate confirmed the appointment, assuming that Chase would support efforts to better the lives of African Americans, a belief that proved accurate. As the war drew to an end, Chase offered his own Reconstruction program. He argued that, during the Civil War, African Americans had proven their loyalty to the Federal government by serving in combat. Blacks had made considerable sacrifice and, accordingly, "simple justice" required that they be enfranchised. After Lincoln's death, Chase tried to influence Andrew Johnson, embarking on an extensive tour of the South to encourage the implementation of his program.[42]

Kinne and Merrick found themselves sympathetic to Chase's argument and serving in an organization that endorsed his goals. The National Freedmen's Relief Association began with objectives that paralleled many freedmen's aid societies. Its teachers believed that education provided avenues to ameliorate many of the harmful effects of slavery. By increasing their knowledge, African Americans could become fully participating citizens. The pursuit of this objective required the creation of common schools to bring together black and white children. The NFRA and its teachers in Florida opened socially integrated facilities in Fernandina, St. Augustine, and Jacksonville during the war. After the war, this policy required personal sacrifices in Gainesville and Lake City. Many teachers were treated as pariahs, and traditional southerners "shrank" from them as if "from a pestilence."[43] In gathering together children of both races at her orphanage, Merrick provoked derogatory comments. As she said, we "bear the reproach, which came from northern as well as southern whites, of being 'n—— teachers'."[44]

While the goals of the NFRA corresponded closely with other aid societies early in the war, some teachers in Virginia backed away from them. The general reluctance of blacks to join the Presbyterian church led to questions about the nature of the African American religious experience. Teachers asked, could they actually be Christians with their inclinations in music and dance? To such doubts were added worries about their behavior. Some teachers came to think of freedmen as being "ignorant, vicious, and degrading."[45] The belief that the negative effects of slavery could be ameliorated gave way to biological racism. Samuel Chapman Armstrong, founder of an important school, identified what he believed to be inherent black traits. "They have low ideas of honor and morality," he concluded, "and a general lack of directive energy, judgment and foresight."[46] From such a perspective, millions of liberated African Americans posed a genuine threat to society in his eyes. Armstrong wrote, "The plastic character of the race put them completely under the control of their leaders. A most unfortunate result of this blind leading the blind is already seen in the belief that political rights are better obtained by political warfare."

Confronted with opinions like these, many progressives feared that social conservatives would use education to prepare freedmen for menial jobs rather than freedom. Education could mold African Americans into a docile, stable work force while teaching them to accept their place at the bottom of southern society.[47] As one historian notes, this agenda helped to produce a curriculum "designed especially for blacks. Major themes included piety, temperance, and character building" rather than academics.[48] Proper behavior ranked as more important than skills meant to enable blacks to compete as citizens.

The different goals of various relief organizations led to polarization. Some aid societies allied themselves with denominations; others remained secular. As both groups appealed for limited resources, they began competing with each other. The outcome of this struggle ultimately had an injurious effect upon African Americans, since the secular societies, which tended to be less conservative, ultimately lost the struggle. As the Civil War ended, though, the results of the conflict were not yet apparent, and the NFRA actually changed from a denominational to a secular society. When Chase began organizing his southern tour in 1865, the aid societies varied in their willingness to assist him. The NFRA stood as the most cooperative.[49]

At that point, Florida politics began to serve Chase's purposes. In coming south, he wanted evidence that his program of enfranchising African Americans could work, a wish that was communicated by Treasury agents. When Kinne learned of the reason for Chase's tour, he set out to augment the efforts of Wesleyan Methodists, the NFRA, and the Chief Justice. In the spring of 1865, Kinne encouraged the formation of a town government for Fernandina, Florida. He wrote, "After the fall of Richmond and the surrender of Lee's army, a committee was appointed which agreed to a plan of action. The only unresolved issue was whether or not the vote should be extended to black men."[50] After a local committee rejected this proposal, Kinne managed to introduce the topic to a larger body. Since African Americans outnumbered whites, the issue was quickly resolved. Kinne observed, "The first vote went one hundred and twenty-three to twenty-seven. . . . Seeing the inevitable, twenty-five traditional southerners left the meeting. A final vote followed, giving unanimous support to black suffrage."[51]

A precedent-setting event soon followed close on the heels of this already momentous step. In an election held on May 1, 1865, 160 voters cast ballots to elect a mayor, a marshal, and eight councilmen. While conservatives boycotted the event, some nine whites joined African Americans in what Kinne described as "the quietest, most unanimous and purest election ever attended."[52] Those opposed to the election pressured the military to ignore it. Their effectiveness proved short-lived when Chase arrived in Fernandina on May 18 and administered the oath of office to Mayor-Elect Adolphus Mot, his children's former French teacher. Major General John Gilmore responded, "I shall issue an order fully recognizing the municipal government of Fernandina."[53] These words signaled Kinne's triumph, and the chief justice obtained his evidence that members of both races could cooperate, voting together. In great enthusiasm Chase inquired of Charles Sumner, "Was that not an event?"[54] An equally pleased Kinne happily informed Syracuse citizens of the news, describing Mot as "the first mayor ever elected in the South by universal suffrage."[55]

While the election's significance failed to be lauded nationally, the victory was celebrated by Merrick, Kinne, and others. Mot remained in office, and the election offered an accurate indicator of future black behavior. If they held the franchise, able to vote, African Americans would ignore the wishes of traditional southerners and pursue their own agendas. This message had implications for anyone interested in politics in the South. In many Florida counties African Americans made up a majority; statewide they represented 47 percent of the overall population. The enfranchisement of blacks meant that local political races could easily be won by Yankee strangers and African Americans. Victories in statewide offices were within reach. Among Florida's whites were a number of Unionists, southerners who had opposed the Confederacy and therefore received ill treatment at its hands. The addition of their votes to those of blacks could yield a majority if a few thousand northerners could be persuaded to move to the state.

The significance of the election was appreciated, though, in Jacksonville, where it confirmed John Sanford Swaim's hopes for a truly emancipated society. It was Swaim who offered reformers an agenda with a strategy for its implementation. In time his influence would reach beyond Harrison Reed and Chloe Merrick to Harriet Beecher Stowe and Charles Beecher.

Civil War Plans to Seize Florida

A series of complicated events preceded Jacksonville's emergence as a center of social reform and the establishment of nearby Mandarin as a residence for Harriet Beecher Stowe. First, though, a closer look should be taken at several other persons who were to figure significantly in future developments. One of them, John Swaim, a prominent Methodist Episcopal minister, stopped in Fernandina in July 1864, before continuing on to his ministerial assignment in Jacksonville. Initially he held the position of a volunteer chaplain, a job whose duties were less taxing than the job's locale. His own poor health was exacerbated by the rough living conditions in Jacksonville. Yet he also discovered new opportunities and met one of the Beechers.

Swaim's background offered the probability of real effectiveness in "liberating" Florida from the shackle hold of its antebellum past. Before illness set in, he had accomplished decades of notable professional achievement. At the age of twenty-eight, he began his ministry in 1834 as a circuit rider in rural New Jersey. As he gained skill, church officials promoted him to more and more extensive circuits. By the 1840s many of his routes served more than 400 congregants. Progress with the circuits was followed by assignments to specific churches in towns whose congregations were considered large at the time.[1] Along with duties in towns came opportunities to serve on local conference committees. In 1850, he was a member of a Committee of Examinations, which tested the knowledge of prospective new ministers. He later served on committees for Sunday Schools (1852), Temperance (1855), and Education (1856, 1861).[2]

By the end of the 1850s, Swaim was acting as the treasurer for the conference. Recognition of his able leadership led to an extraordinary honor. In 1856, his conference chose him to be a representative at the General Assembly meeting in Indianapolis. The Methodist Episcopal Church was the nation's largest and wealthiest Protestant denomination at that time, and major decisions were the prerogative of this powerful body. John Swaim became one of 217 persons nationwide representing millions of Methodists. From this peak his career ebbed as he tended to a daughter's ill health and became saddled with his own lingering illness. In the early 1860s Mary Swaim returned to her parents' home, no longer able to serve as a faculty member at a seminary in Pennington, New Jersey. Struggling with consumption, she lived until October 7, 1862. By the spring of 1864, John Swaim was classified among the inactive clergy. In eight years he had gone from the General Assembly to the disabled list.[3]

During this dark period came the chance for Swaim to serve in the South, and he responded. Rather than following Mary's pattern of staying in the North, he hoped the warmer climate would offer potential for recovery. When he received Bishop Edmund S. Janes's assignment to preach to Federal troops and freed blacks in Jacksonville, he made preparations for a permanent move. Whatever difficulties awaited him in the South, the future offered hope. From a distance the situation seemed manageable, especially since his wife, Catherine, and brother-in-law, Wesley Robertson, were to join him.[4]

When Swaim arrived in Jacksonville, though, he found a town in disarray, occupied by demoralized Union troops. Federal troops were holding the town after three previous temporary visits. An earlier occupation had been followed by a rampage during which an angry mob had burned the businesses of prominent Unionists. The conflagration destroyed six blocks and some twenty-five buildings. The town's most important businessman, Calvin Robinson, narrowly escaped; this was to have a lasting consequence later. News of these events added fuel to the already widely circulated reports about Confederate abuse of Florida Unionists. Agents of Salmon Chase, in turn, used these accounts to criticize Lincoln.

Under pressure from Chase's supporters, the army seized the town on February 7, 1864, and prepared to drive Confederate forces from the state. This ambitious plan coincided with the visit of the president's personal secretary, John Hay—dispatched to Florida to measure the strength of Unionist sentiment. Hay could not complete his task because General Truman Seymour engaged a quickly assembled Confederate force near Olustee on February 20, only to be decisively repulsed. Thereafter, additional troops reinforced Jacksonville's garrison, as new fortifications protected the town.[5]

Coincidentally, when Swaim arrived in Jacksonville, Colonel James Chapman Beecher lived in a railroad water tank at Baldwin, twenty miles away. James, like all of his brothers, had been raised for the ministry rather than the army. He claimed that his father would "pray him into it." Yet, as with his older half brother Charles, years went by before those prayers were answered. Sent to Dartmouth at sixteen, he there created a furor by criticizing the curriculum and was suspended for this sedition. After a period of suspension, though, he returned to Dartmouth in 1848 and graduated at the age of twenty.

Upon leaving college, Beecher went to sea rather than comply with his father's wishes to join the ministry. A family member wrote, "For five years he was in the East India trade, shipping first as a common sailor and later as an officer on the fastest and the most beautiful sailing ships which ever sailed the seas."[6] After this stint he returned to the United States and enrolled in Andover Theological Seminary. A request to take charge of the Seamen's Bethel at Hong Kong interrupted his studies, asserted Lyman Stowe: "With his experience, this was just the place for him so he was hurriedly ordained as a minister, and set sail for China."[7] With the outbreak of the Civil War, Beecher returned home and "enlisted as the chaplain of the First Long Island Regiment."[8] Finding these duties uninteresting, he requested an assignment as an officer and so before coming south he served as a captain and a lieutenant-colonel.

The youngest of Lyman Beecher's children recruited freedmen near New Bern, North Carolina, in May and June 1863. "Within six weeks," a family member wrote, he organized a regiment, the First North Carolina Volunteers, and had it "uniformed, armed, and handsomely en-camped."[9] The training he gave the regiment evidently was effective since this unit performed with distinction at the battle of Olustee, joining the Fifty-fourth Massachusetts "to save the army." The credit for this performance went to the African American troops and Beecher's staff, for he was not present. Instead, he was away in the North looking for arms when his troops were ordered to Jacksonville. He did not catch up with them until after the fight.

Having sought combat, Beecher fumed at having narrowly missed it. News of Olustee came to him "suddenly" and "the shock" left him briefly "unbalanced."[10] Engaged to Frances "Frankie" Johnson, he wanted to be with his troops but also wanted to be with her. It was with a mixture of emotions that he arrived in Jacksonville on March 11, 1864. Once in the town, he borrowed a horse and rode out to his regiment. Spotted by his soldiers, he was "rushed," and his agitation melted. "Such ringing cheers," he wrote Frankie. "Such crowding. God bless 'em. They knew I wanted to be with them."[11] Beecher's fears that he could not be close to his fiancée were equally unfounded, and they soon made plans for mar-riage. The ceremony was held in Jacksonville in July and included the participation of a general's staff, African Americans, and the music of the Seventh U.S. military band, which gave the newlyweds an evening ser-enade. "Dramatic in sight and sound," Frankie exclaimed, as she said "that sorrow" had "left the earth forever."[12]

The delightful ceremony preceded Beecher's assignment to take his troops to guard Baldwin, a small railroad junction and the site of his makeshift residence, a railroad water tank. He went alone, leaving Frankie in Jacksonville. During the next month, his soldiers suffered illnesses caused by living near swamps. This gave him cause for anxiety and despair. Sleepless nights in his quarters left him feeling "stupid and soulless." Asking for help, he wrote that God could make his officers "efficient." God could turn the ordnance department into more than a "nuisance." God could fill the growing "vacancies" in his ranks. He confessed to Frankie in Jacksonville, "If I only could work without worry."[13]

Frankie Beecher responded to his plight by sending letters and visiting him in Baldwin. Decades later she recalled trips on a railroad "platform car, escorted by the assistant adjutant general, the provost marshal, and others. The officers and enlisted men spied right and left for the enemy, stopping the train to hear the reports of the scouts."[14] Although these temporary visits lightened his sense of despair, James Beecher found ongoing relief by being reassigned to Jacksonville in August—an event that he and Frankie celebrated. On August 28, he jubilantly preached to his troops. Private Justus Silliman observed in his diary, "I listened to an excellent sermon from Col. James C. Beecher. His text was Philippians: 3, verses 13–14. He used no notes and spoke in a conversational style. His sermon was well delivered and its teaching plain so that the simplest could understand."[15] That day, James filled in for John Swaim.

Private Silliman at the time was helping Swaim by teaching in the schools; he wrote to his mother of Swaim's difficulties. The few remaining conservatives gave "him the cold shoulder," and discussions with "influential citizens" revealed "deep rooted prejudice."[16] Rather than offering Swaim sympathy, they created problems, especially resisting integrated services. According to the soldier, the minister responded by scheduling three different Sunday services: one at 10:30 or 11:00 "for the special benefit of white citizens which did not entirely shut the Negro from attending; at three in the afternoon he preaches for the benefit of the Negro though whites are cordially invited. In the evening the discourse is intended for both black and white, so there is no excuse for not attending."[17]

Silliman's letters also reveal a pattern of inconsistent vigor to Swaim's life. At times illness prevented Swaim from preaching; on one occasion the soldier found the church closed and the minister "very feeble." At other times Swaim rallied, and by the time Catherine Swaim came in late September, he had purchased a large house. As he supervised repairs on the dwelling, the condition of his brother-in-law became a heavy burden. Upon his arrival in August 1864, Robertson had disguised his poor health with "lively" cheerfulness. But he then contracted typhoid fever, with which he suffered for days. Eventually the care given to him seemed to work, and he improved until late October, only to relapse and die on November 2. This experience took a dreadful toll on both John and Catherine. When Swaim preached, a historian observed that "a man little given to public displays of emotion showed none at all."[18]

In spite of this tragedy, Swaim made wise decisions. His new home met family needs with rooms left over, so they chose to board guests, which gave the family an immediate source of income as well as a guaranteed livelihood should hostile southerners reject his ministry. Using family resources, he and Catherine expeditiously appointed their home with items not commonly found in wartime Jacksonville residences. When Silliman called on them in October, he found the house "neatly fixed" and an oasis of civilization: "It was there that I first stepped into a carpeted room since leaving New York, so you may well imagine that I appreciated the privilege."[19]

The opening of the boardinghouse brought guests and new friends. Soon to follow Silliman would come Harrison Reed, Chloe Merrick, Ansel Kinne, and teachers who had enlisted in the North to teach African Americans. While schools, politics, and the war were the most frequent topics of conversation, the agricultural potential of this new place was also noted. The climate could permit crops to grow when the weather further north would make it unthinkable. Such conversations gave rise to speculation and the seeds of action.

During the times when James Beecher occasionally filled in for Swaim, Frankie Beecher was taking in the sights. She wrote about "the wonderful colors" of the "miniature lakes of Greencove Springs" and watched "sunsets that surpass those of Italy" from a boat on the St. Johns River. At times, her husband joined her, and they scurried "like children released from school."[20] And on Thanksgiving the Beechers were able to enjoy a wild turkey, while the Swaims shared pork, potatoes, and a large duff (flour pudding) with Silliman.

This idyllic period ended on Thanksgiving evening with the arrival of orders for the regiment to depart for South Carolina, leaving an anxious

Frankie in Jacksonville with a small garrison and lots of extra military equipment. For the next ten days she heard nothing, and when news came it was shocking. James lay in a hospital bed, having been wounded three times while leading his troops at Honey Hill. He learned after the war that Confederate soldiers were surprised he survived, since their officers gave orders to aim at him. Recuperating in a hospital in Beaufort, he wrote Frankie a few lines asking her to come, and she sped to him on the next ship. Over the next four weeks she stayed nearby, and he eventually returned to his regiment.[21]

With the war becoming more active in the Carolinas, the couple spent the rest of their time in the South above Savannah. Being part of a family that corresponded regularly, the Beechers in the northeast knew of James's military service. Even though grandsons of Lyman Beecher fought in the Civil War, few surpassed the bravery of his youngest son. Having been "wounded in the thigh at noon," he led his troops until dusk.[22] Still other honors followed this distinction. In April 1865, the army promoted him to a brevet brigadier general and gave him time to visit his half brother in Charleston. James, Frankie, and Henry Ward Beecher watched the "re-raising of the flag of Fort Sumter" on April 14.[23]

Harriet Beecher Stowe also followed James's military career. Earlier, as a token of her esteem, she had helped the women of New Bern design and make the regimental flag. The blue silk banner with "a rising Sun of Liberty" and the words "God is our Sun and Shield" aided recruiting and inspired troops in combat.[24] Its presence at Olustee and at Honey Hill was not unnoted by the famous author. Florida and its mild climate came up in family discussions, and after the war the topic came up again. Stowe's son, Frederick, suffered from the effects of war wounds, and his inability to handle alcohol became a problem for all. A cousin and several friends followed up their military service by inviting Fred to join them in renting a cotton plantation in the state.

While Frankie and James were in the Carolinas, an important visitor arrived at the Swaims' home—Rev. Timothy Willard Lewis, a Presiding Elder of the Methodist Episcopal Church. Lewis headed a district that included the Sea Islands of South Carolina and Georgia and the parts of

Florida in Federal control. Having lived in the South much longer than Swaim, he had formed harsher opinions about traditional southerners: "They loathe our Northern idea of liberty and equal rights before the law."[25] As a consequence, the northern Methodist church would not be attractive to them. He concluded that "the colored people will form the only material for the Methodist Episcopal church as a rule."[26] Within the span of decades, he predicted, "death and immigration" would change the South. Death would remove intolerant southerners, and immigration would bring in northerners who were more flexible.

The logic of this message fit Swaim's experiences and his growing mistrust of local residents. The war had radically altered his thinking. At Indianapolis in 1856, he had presented a memorial that requested that the church avoid a stronger stand on slavery. In his lifetime the Methodist Episcopal church divided on several major occasions. African Americans in the north had broken off to form the African Methodist Episcopal Church, or AME, and the African Methodist Episcopal Church, Zion. Then in 1844, the Methodist Episcopal Church had split over the ownership of slaves. When this happened, southerners formed the M.E. Church, South, and every member of the Annual Conference in Florida joined it. At Indianapolis a proposal submitted by abolitionists was intended to exclude any person "implicated" with slavery. Such a regulation threatened to split the church yet again, and John Swaim had voted with the majority who rejected it.

When the war began, northern Methodist leaders sided with the Federal government, and as the conflict increased, they became more vocal. By 1862, Swaim's own conference described southern leaders as a "heartless and aggressive aristocracy."[27] Historian Robert Williams recounts, "A year later, in the spring of 1863, the conference deemed slavery to be 'unmethodistic' and 'contrary to the teachings of the Gospel'. By the close of the war, the Conference brought disciplinary proceedings against a minister who did not favor abolition."[28] Swaim supported this decision, for his own views had changed.

As the Federal government's war effort neared victory, leaders in the national M.E. Church felt vindicated. They supported the victor and the M.E. Church, South, had lost. One historian observed, "Based upon church policy promulgated during and soon after the Civil War, Methodist ministers from the North involved themselves in every aspect of Reconstruction life—religion, education, civil rights, economic development, and politics."[29] A concern for the well-being of African Americans added to the notion that the northern church should confront its southern rival in the South. Yet, in spite of calls for the participation of northern ministers, only a few responded. The same historian suggested that "the rock bottom guess was fifty" who joined the southern districts of the M.E. Church. Such a small staff forced the church to hire southerners, "many of whom were Unionists."[30]

This practice, according to writers, did not lead to an equal distribution of power since Yankees held presiding elderships and pastorates of the largest churches. Swaim was, of course, one such minister and strengthened his position through personal relationships with bishops. For instance, he actively corresponded with Bishop Baker, and in 1866 received bank drafts for almost $4,000—a significant amount of money in "a cash-starved economy." His connections with the church hierarchy gave Swaim a mandate to act and a position far more powerful than that of most of the other northern clergy.[31]

Events in Jacksonville reinforced this new attitude and eliminated many of the differences between him and more ardent abolitionists such as the Merricks and Kinnes. In April 1865, the Confederacy released the last of the Andersonville prisoners at Baldwin. According to Swaim's account, "News of Union prisoners reached Jacksonville on April 28, and a train was dispatched to bring them into town."[32] When the train returned, the appearance of the soldiers shocked everyone: "They had been exposed to the weather and to 'smoke from pitch pine fires'." Months and years of such treatment had turned their skin black. "Their 'wretchedness' was further accentuated by an 'absence of razors and of combs and brushes'." The poor quality of their clothing, as Swaim wrote, did nothing to help their appearance: "Some were without shirts and others had no pants. 'Not a few' wore only a very shabby pair of drawers."[33]

While some relief came quickly—the men bathed in the river, and the army issued new uniforms—undoing damaged health took much longer. The symptoms of scurvy abounded. "Sore and swollen feet" were com-

mon, and one poor man "had a portion of his face eaten away." John
Swaim responded by helping in every way he could; he answered questions about the war and Union victories and distributed a thousand en-
velopes so that letters could be written home. When soldiers exhausted
his stationery, he begged local merchants for more. While most of the
former prisoners of war soon left the South, two hundred remained in
Jacksonville, too ill to travel. Within two weeks thirty died and Swaim
was performing their funerals. "Their deaths were a blow" to the old
minister. "It is sad to know," he wrote, "that so many, after enduring
terrible treatment, should die, just now, as they were beginning to have
the hope of seeing home."[34]

Rather than sinking into despair, Swaim allowed his thoughts to be
tempered by a vision of a new future—a vision that would influence other
reformers, including Harriet Beecher Stowe. A few months earlier in
1865, his ideas had coalesced. He modified the ideas of Timothy Willard
Lewis by planning to change the speed of immigration. If the rate of
immigration to the South could be considerably hastened, then a very
different South could be created in the state of Florida. Yankees could be
attracted to the state by replaying variations on old agricultural themes
such as cotton and by offering opportunities to invest in new economic
ventures. A few orange groves along the river suggested one answer; yet
another came from reports of the successful growing and harvesting of
vegetables in the early spring. If steamships were to transport the produce to market in New York before it arrived from any other place,
fortunes could be made. The mild winter climate surely could attract the
many sufferers of consumption. Even if they originally came as tourists
or short-term visitors, with these enticements they might be convinced
to stay.

Swaim's plan required an influx of Yankee residents from which to
recruit permanent citizens. The addition of a few thousand such settlers
could alter the future balance of power between African Americans and
traditional southerners. The white majority (4,366 in 1870) was actually
smaller than the census suggested, since many of the 2,000 to 3,000
Unionists opposed former Confederate leaders. With the addition of

new Yankee residents to the Unionists and enfranchised blacks, Florida could be controlled democratically. Swaim wrote, "we want to out vote" traditional southerners "and hold them as a helpless minority." "Then we can manage things for the real advantage of the country."[35]

The success of such a coalition would result in benefits for each of the participating groups. African Americans, Swaim thought, would gain as free laborers in a dynamic economy and as elected public officials. At the same time, by sharing power, Unionists and Yankees would have political strength far in excess of their numbers, something that would protect them and their economic interests from the whims of traditional southerners. The latter group, he thought, would be sure to offer complaints bitterly, yet in time the power of the new order would overwhelm them. Such a future, however, required serious educational change. Before the war the state legally denied an education to African Americans and allocated meager funds even for white children. Between July 1853 and July 1854, for instance, Florida allotted $5,031.07 to educate its 16,577 white children, just over thirty cents per child. Such a budget never supported free public education, and the state "distributed its funds among the teachers of private schools."[36] Future participation in a democracy would require substantive educational change, especially since the economy would be dynamic and holding of public office would be important, requiring an educated citizenry.

Swaim brought these pieces together in his dream of a free and vibrant Florida. It would be based upon democratic ideas and founded upon an economy of tourism and Yankee residents—people with investments in citrus and novel crops. Such ideas were not just airy speculation. Fellow clergymen remembered him as having a "keen, logical intellect." They described him elsewhere as "a man of more than ordinary intelligence."[37]

In 1865 Swaim set out to realize his dream with a publicity campaign. To that end he wrote letters and sent them to the *Newark Sentinel of Freedom*. This newspaper promptly published his April 12th description of the St. Johns River, an article that showcased state attractions. He told readers that "the production of fruit" began south of Jacksonville. Mandarin, Swaim observed, "furnishes a pretty good supply of oranges for our place" and even more could be gotten from groves near Palatka. Further west, toward the center of the state, "is a most splendid country."[38] While formerly this region served as a source of supplies for the Confederacy, Swaim predicted it would "become a garden."[39] One could "not estimate the quantity of cotton, sugar, oranges, lemons, bananas, pineapples, and early garden vegetables that might be furnished to our northern market." To this he added the notion that in Florida a person could go to a garden on every day of the year and find something "appropriate to the season." If Yankees had not imagined the resources of the region, Swaim would enlighten them.

In less than two weeks, on April 21, John Swaim posted yet another letter and the newspaper published it. In this description of Jacksonville, he tantalized northerners with the town's "delightful" location: "From the wharfs on Bay or River Street the view is exceedingly beautiful, the river presenting its broad surface for many miles. Occasionally, [there is] a jutting headland or promontory, large enough for a splendid plantation, with sufficient improvements to make a delightful and even magnificent island-like home."[40] In this account he identified the various trees that flourished in the town and the contents of a nearby garden. There "are a great variety of flowers and shrubs," which he indicated had an extraordinary potential. They could produce "a bouquet" on "each day of the year."[41] For those interested, he noted "roses in endless varieties; lilies such as they cultivate in the North with great care, flaunting their beauties and shedding their fragrance." Then he recounted the destruction that had been inflicted upon the city. To reassure investors, he advised: "Improvement is the order of the day and everything points to the speedy resuscitation of the town."[42]

Yet another article appeared on May 16, published just two days before Salmon Chase swore in the mayor of Fernandina. In it Swaim gave his account of the Andersonville prisoners and their treatment by Confederate authorities. The wretched condition of the soldiers had been produced by poor diet and a minuscule ration of soap. Imagine, as Swaim recorded, living on "two inches of bad bacon and a pint of coarsely ground corn meal, cob and all."[43] Try staying outdoors without protection from rain, frost, or hail, with only a "spoonful of soap" a week. Bugs infested the soldier's deplorable clothing, and, while the men bathed in the river, it was thrown into heaps and burned.

Like its predecessors Swaim's third article also received special treatment. The *Newark Sentinel of Freedom* printed the story and ran it again in its subsidiary, the *Newark Daily Advertiser.* This practice not only rewarded Swaim's efforts but doubled their effect. The press interest in Florida could be explained by a number of prewar connections between the states. For instance, the local Federal judge, Philip Fraser, was from Elizabeth, New Jersey. Fraser had served as mayor of Jacksonville before the war, as had Obadiah Congar, also from northern New Jersey. Congar's niece, Catherine, came from Newark and was the wife of prominent Jacksonville resident and Unionist leader Ossian B. Hart. Such linkages assured that articles about Florida would be read with interest.[44]

News of the election orchestrated by Kinne in Fernandina no doubt reached Swaim. Salmon P. Chase arrived in Jacksonville on May 20, 1865. Word of the new government in Fernandina confirmed Swaim's hopes. His dream of a Yankee state in southern climes, the newspaper articles, and proof of multiracial cooperation came together as if by divine inspiration. The extraordinary coalescing of events was not mere coincidence for Rev. John Sanford Swaim. The unfolding scenario may have evoked the words of the writer of Revelation, "Behold a new heaven and a new earth." Swaim envisioned a means for the economic development of Florida and a strategy for its implementation. Within a few years other reformers would join him in this effort, including Harriet Beecher Stowe. Before then, however, he faced Presidential Reconstruction, a period that might have vexed even the author of the last book of the Bible.

Sphinx at the Gate of Thebes

Presidential Reconstruction

Presidential Reconstruction created unexpected difficulties for social reformers, altering their fortunes before the arrival of Harriet Beecher Stowe. Problems also arose from traditional southerners who returned to their homes at the end of the Civil War, bringing vastly different experiences and ideas, harboring a wide range of sentiments. Some had merely endured the war and only wanted to be left alone to rebuild their lives. Still others sought to restore the old social and political order and told freedmen that they would "still be slaves in some way."[1] As former Florida Senator David Levy Yulee explained, the South must have "some form of compulsory labor" or be "Africanized and ruined."[2] Such words alarmed Merrick, Kinne, and the NFRA, lending credence to the notion that many southerners had not really changed. Such fears were soon heightened by the actions of President Andrew Johnson. At first he did not reveal the form of Reconstruction he preferred. A season of advice-giving followed Lincoln's death, in which those who wanted to be president, including Salmon Chase, sought Johnson's ear, as did the civic-minded of every direction.[3]

This period ended with the president's proclamations on May 29, 1865—actions that disrupted the dreams of reformers. The ensuing documents authorized the issuing of pardons to Confederate sympathizers, restoring their rights while ignoring the status of freedmen. Such actions meant that Chase's mission to the South had failed. The chief justice ended his effort to influence Johnson. News of the president's decision also had other effects, leaving Adolphus Mot, the newly elected mayor of Fernandina, for example, without a base of support. Concerned, his discomfort increased with the knowledge that Chase no longer controlled the patronage of the Treasury Department. The political machine was falling apart; in frustration he wrote the chief justice: "The proclamation of the President on State reconstruction stands in the path of future history like a sphinx at the gate of Thebes, offering problems to be solved, enigmas and secrets to be derived. It is proclaimed that States shall be provided with a republican form of government by the votes of loyal citizens. What form? Is the freedman a citizen? Shall he vote? Will oath and testimony make southern men loyal? Should reconstruction be left at the hands of prejudiced southern men? What form of government can be expected but the Confederate States of America pattern of Oligarchical republics?"[4]

Mot's fears were not unfounded. Florida's provisional governor, William Marvin, called for a constitutional convention in the fall of 1865. One historian recounts, "After hearing him proclaim that 'the governing power is in the hands of the white race' that body met the President's minimum requirements for readmission to the union."[5] Elections for governor and legislature followed in November. The newly elected governor, David S. Walker, opened his administration by pursuing a series of regulations to control African Americans. A sympathetic legislature quickly passed laws largely reinstituting slavery. Within six months of Mot's letter, the oligarchical republics reappeared across the states of the old Confederacy. As those once in power recovered it, they also sought control of land. They petitioned Andrew Johnson, in writing and in person, for property sold at tax sales and for buildings occupied by the military. The president responded sympathetically, and it became policy to return real estate to southerners. At the same time, he ignored his administration's promises to African Americans. They did not receive the promised forty acres and a mule, and the farms created by their toil were returned to their oppressors.

Rather than helping former slaves, one of the leaders of the Freedman's Bureau in Florida, Thomas W. Osborn, placed an early priority on the return of property. This policy stripped aid societies of the buildings they were using, usually before these facilities could be replaced.[6] The decision led to conflict with reformers, and struggles with Osborn plagued the reformers (including Charles Beecher) for years to come. As one would have expected, Ansel Kinne and the NFRA vigorously opposed Osborn and his plans. This opposition became especially intense when an Episcopal priest returned to Fernandina and sought possession of the local sanctuary. After having been abandoned in 1862, the church had been given by the military to Chloe Merrick and Cornelia Smith for their use as a school. Later, when other teachers had followed in their stead, Kinne maintained the building. Writing to Osborn, Kinne "pleaded for relief": "I hope you will not be in great haste to return the church. If it could be [kept] for its present purpose [it will] do much good." Far better, he maintained, than anything done by "all of the disloyal preachers in the country."[7]

Osborn, however, preferred to cultivate political relationships with many southerners, and he ignored Kinne. Such actions, in turn, encouraged former Confederate General Joseph Finegan to reclaim his house in Fernandina—the location of Merrick's orphanage. Finegan's efforts were blocked for a while by both Chloe Merrick and Ansel Kinne. Realizing Osborn's lack of sympathy, they turned to the NFRA's leaders and enlisted its president to appeal directly to the head of the Freedmen's Bureau. This tactic eventually failed because it came to be in conflict with presidential policy. On July 6, 1866, the Freedmen's Bureau ordered the orphanage to be moved south of Jacksonville.[8]

This decision added to the uncertainty about the orphanage's future existence. In spite of a Rebel general's telling Merrick that "he knew of at least five hundred orphan children in this State," there seemed little official interest in helping.[9] Merrick sought consolation in the notion that "the children of slavery's degradation had quickened into new life."[10] Few southerners, however, valued her or her accomplishments. Since Emma Kinne also worked at the orphanage, its future would profoundly affect the Kinne household. As Presidential Reconstruction continued, new NFRA teachers received assignments to schools in the interior of Florida. Ansel Kinne helped them as they faced the hostility of southerners. In the first half of 1866, he visited Jacksonville on eight different occasions, often in transit to other places.[11] During May alone he went to Tallahassee, Gainesville, and Lake City.

In his travels he found that pressure on the teachers did not deter them from continuing to teach and to mix socially with African American families. A teacher wrote, "Last night we were invited to a tea party where two or three of our scholars lived. As we had never been there, we were wondering what sort of a place we should find, as some of their cabins are not very desirable places to eat one's supper, but we were ushered into quite a neat house. We were entertained mostly by a tall, stately black woman, until tea, when we sat around the table which was full of good things with them, they expressing much gratitude that they enjoyed this privilege, saying, 'A few years ago we should not have dared to do this'."[12]

Unlike some of the aid society workers in Virginia, the NFRA teachers continued to promote academic subjects. The teachers emphasized geography, arithmetic, spelling, and reading.[13] In Gainesville one had an advanced student in grammar beyond the primary department. Rather than retreating into biological racism, NFRA teachers noted student progress: "They advance, and whatever knowledge they acquire is by hard study. I can boast of some very smart, ambitious scholars, with good heads and good hearts, too. I am free to say that I am proud of them."[14]

The NFRA responded to Merrick's and Kinne's problems with Osborn by ordering all of its teachers and staff in Florida to report to Kinne. This decision meant that they were to ignore Osborn and his superintendent of education. As a consequence, neither man knew details of school operations.[15] Such a decision gave little comfort to Kinne, who was coping with a significant administrative responsibility. From the two teachers sent in 1862, Merrick and Smith, the entire system grew by June 1866 to "thirteen schools, one orphanage, twenty-seven teachers, and 1,663 students."

While Kinne struggled with Osborn, African Americans focused their anger upon Governor Walker's black codes and the legislature's reinvention of slavery. A public gathering in Fernandina blasted state leaders, and not long afterward, hundreds of freedmen marched at Quincy to demand their rights. Church leaders also expressed strong feelings on these issues. AME Bishop Henry McNeal Turner said, "I shall neither fawn nor cringe nor stoop to beg for my rights."[16] Demands for change in Florida were repeated in other places, and confrontations in Memphis and New Orleans succeeded in turning national public opinion against Johnson's policies. The election of former Confederate generals to state offices only added to the outrages perpetrated upon African Americans. By the summer of 1866, a historian writes, "the situation had grown so severe" in Florida that authorities proclaimed martial law in five counties. The excesses of Presidential Reconstruction fueled a political firestorm for Johnson—one that few presidents could imagine.[17]

Following the orphanage's move, Chloe Merrick refocused her attention on the needs of its children. Poor health, however, soon overwhelmed these concerns. Only at the end of the year did she recover enough strength to travel, returning north to her family in Syracuse to recuperate. In 1867 Merrick sought a new teaching assignment in the South. The orphanage closed and authorities dispersed its children, who were either apprenticed or sent to facilities in the Carolinas. Going to the Carolinas appealed to Chloe herself, and she began teaching in Columbia, South Carolina, and then in New Bern, North Carolina.

At this time, the NFRA and other secular aid societies continued their losing battle with the denominational aid societies. As the secular organizations were forced out of black education, funding for the NFRA declined. For a while it survived by transferring much of the financial responsibility to African American communities. By 1869, in Jacksonville, the NFRA leaders paid "only the salaries of the teachers while the [local] people provided for their board."[18] As Merrick watched this process, she came to reject the use of philanthropy to meet the needs of African Americans. Charity, she wrote, "is inadequate as a permanent system": "Even as a 'temporary expedient', it harmed blacks when it treated them as 'dependents'." African Americans were not "wards but citizens—citizens with both 'rights' and 'responsibilities'."[19]

While Merrick, Kinne, and the NFRA struggled, John Swaim used his publishing success to continue to trumpet the lures of the state. On

August 19, 1865, he wrote his fourth newspaper article—one that noted economic recovery in Jacksonville. Within weeks of the end of the war, merchants restocked their stores to "utmost capacity." Business proved brisk as planters purchased goods for the interior, and great quantities of cotton were shipped. "Huge piles" littered the wharves, and Swaim reported that the state had some 75,000 bales at the end of the conflict. The size of these shipments led to much speculation. Swaim wryly asked, Was this "not the very cotton that was burned to prevent Yankees from getting it?"[20]

Planters also turned to contracting with former slaves to resume work on their farms. The success of these negotiations depended upon the character of white farmers. Those known for being "cruel" often found themselves without laborers. African Americans were unwilling to accept, Swaim reported, the "same old plantation slang" and the "same imperious voices."[21] They resisted "indignity" and went to places that offered better treatment. With the departure of the able-bodied, the worst of the planters turned upon the elderly and disabled who lingered. Swaim learned that "some were pettish and sullen and drove them off the plantations." After such events economic reality set in. Planters began selling their farms at bargain prices. Swaim knew of one consisting of 4,400 acres, and he published a thorough description. It had "a splendid dwelling and out-buildings, cotton gin and sugar mill, with the crops growing—all for twenty thousand dollars."[22] Still another could be bought for one dollar an acre. Swaim, always the promoter, then added, "The chances for a young man of limited means are better here in Florida than in any portion of the South."[23]

Swaim concluded his August article by sharing part of his dream: "Let a colony come down and purchase a tract sufficient to give each family a farm of one hundred acres." Within a short period of time, he maintained, "they could be surrounded with every appliance of comfort and all of the tropical fruits raised with little labor or cost." He added what was for him the most important point: "In this manner a virtuous and prosperous and an intelligent population would soon control this 'Italy of America'."[24]

In the spring of 1866, the minister wrote two more articles to attract Yankees. These works described a long trip that took him and Ansel Kinne from Jacksonville to Sumterville, some fifty miles northeast of Tampa. Using a light buggy and a mule, they rode through miles of yellow pine forest to Middleburg—a small town that most residents had abandoned. Then they traveled west and followed the path of the Florida Railroad to Gainesville. From Gainesville they proceeded to Micanopy and Ocala, "a fine looking country town." As they journeyed southwest from Ocala, the woods became "emphatically wild." Sumterville turned out to be eight or nine buildings in "the original forest." Swaim found "the court house to be unpainted and dilapidated; two stores and some five dwellings, all without paint or even whitewash."[25]

While the innkeeper prepared dinner at a rudely constructed "hotel," Kinne and Swaim watched the distillation of whiskey. Having heard of the local product, they "had a curiosity to see how it was made." Swaim "found a large iron pot of some six gallons, set in a very rude clay furnace, standing out to the weather—no roof or shed to cover it. For a covering, a half of what had been a butter firkin was turned upon it, clay being packed between its lower edge and the rim of the pot to prevent the escape of steam. Near the top of this covering the end of a reed was inserted, the other end [passing through] a huge cypress water trough, some eight to ten feet long, and coming out the other end."[26] Jugs collected condensed liquid, and near the still an old barrel stood holding a fermented mass. The countenance of Swaim's host convinced him of the power of the "beverage."

Completing their visit, the two men retraced their journey to Ocala and proceeded to Silver Springs, "one of the many wonders of Florida." As they approached it, the pines gave way to live oaks and "tall magnolias, and the slim trunks of cabbage palms closely crowded together and all hung with long festoons of gray moss pendants."[27] Swaim found the spring in the center of these solemn surroundings, some 160 to 200 feet wide and some 60 to 80 feet deep. "Out of wide chasms in the limestone rock," he wrote, flow "abundant waters with perfect naturalness; so pure and transparent that a sixpence could be seen distinctively. The fishes, the pebbles, even the sands appear, and there is just sulfur and magnesia enough in the water to tinge everything with a silver hue. When one looks down into these depths with his back to the sun, the most gorgeous prismatic colors are seen in every possible shade, constantly changing like the flashes of the Aurora Borealis."[28]

From this extraordinary place they rode to Orange Springs, some twenty miles away, and then to Palatka. Swaim found the town in ruins. "Many pleasant homes have been burned and some are falling down and despoiled."[29] Yet these losses and the suffering it created had not changed attitudes. Local people did not see that "secession and treason were either an evil or a wrong. Many of those suffering are heard to say that they had but a single regret concerning the rebellion, that is that it did not succeed. And yet the all absorbing subject of thought and conversation among these persons is, of what they were 'before the war'. They never wasted their substance in a terrible and bootless war, no!" Now they spent their time blaming others, saying, "The Yankees stole everything."[30] Swaim found this ludicrous and believed that, on the contrary, many of their difficulties resulted from their own actions, the larger part of which had been folly. Swaim asserted that it would have been "more manly" if they just "confessed!"

Ansel Kinne's account of this trip also includes a candid assessment of southern attitudes. Many southerners did not want help. They wished to be left "alone" in the devastation war had wrought. According to the educator, "public opinion is set against any and all efforts on the part of northern individuals and associations, to ameliorate or reconstruct.[31] Kinne thought they might accept financial help, but only if it were offered with the understanding that these people "were not poor in spirit." He concluded that ignorance reinforced pride and poverty. Before the war they lived "without a school system."[32]

While many conditions among poor whites were as bad as those among blacks, the situation of the latter was better than Kinne expected. He wrote, "Instead of finding them wandering from place to place, or idling, they were generally employed on plantations, in mechanical labor, or as house servants."[33] In 1865 workers and planters divided many of the crops, something that appeared to meet the need for food. Some shortages, however, arose at the end of the war. With the prospect of freedom, many African Americans reduced their labor in the fields—a trend that affected crop production. Even so, Kinne believed, "good crops were realized and whenever the division was equitably made the share given to the freedmen enabled them to subsist for the present year."[34] The presence of laborers, as Swaim had reported earlier, reflected the treatment of African Americans. When landowners acted fairly, freedmen responded with diligent work. When planters were brutal or unfair, their "fields were doomed to be uncultivated." Such justice came swiftly since the knowledge of working conditions traveled. "Negroes," said one planter, "have a kind of telegraph by which they know all about the treatment of Negroes on the plantations for a great distance around."[35]

While Kinne placed confidence in the ability of African Americans, their future seemed uncertain. If the prejudice and hate were to subside, the educator believed that conditions among blacks "would rapidly improve." Genuine freedom would act as a stimulant, yielding many positive developments. For this to happen, Kinne felt, the friends of African Americans, those "who believe in his humanity," would have to act. Blacks needed help in "pushing aside that prejudice that jeopardizes their rights."[36]

After Kinne and Swaim returned to Jacksonville, the minister modified his ministry to meet emerging conditions. With the end of the war, the government disbanded military units, and the population in the town changed. On February 18, 1866, Swaim and Timothy Willard Lewis helped to organize the remaining black members of the M.E. church into a congregation. The election of trustees followed on May 8. These included one white, Calvin Robinson, and three African Americans. Some of the success of this venture reflected the minister's cordial relationship with the black community. Rather than imposing his own wishes, as did some missionaries in places such as Virginia, he consulted African Americans. When he looked for a lot for the church sanctuary, Swaim sought the advice of a local minister, Lymas Anders.[37] Months later, when he proposed action on another matter, the African American trustees thought otherwise and stopped him. With reluctance Swaim observed, "We could not do what we wanted."[38]

In the last half of May and first part of June 1866, John Swaim supervised the construction of the church building. Work began with the laying of brick pilings and the purchase of building supplies. "When problems developed because the carpenters 'cut the wrong stuff'," Swaim caught the mistake and prevented major delays. The minister wrote, "By June 15, the rafters were in, and the workers 'went to boarding up the gable ends'."[39] Less than ten days later he recorded, "I went and opened Sunday School in the new church. There were 18 males and 31 females." Sunday School was followed by three different services, one in the morning, another at 3:00 in the afternoon, and a third in the evening. Significantly, Swaim shared the pulpit that day with local blacks, including Louis Wright, the church's steward.[40] This was not unique behavior on his part. He dined with blacks in Charleston on April 3, 1866, in Jacksonville on May 2, and in Gainesville on October 20. It is also revealing that when he rode in the rain with a local black preacher, Ned Stewart, both men took turns riding upon a wagon.[41]

While furthering the cause of integration, he also helped NFRA teachers. An 1865 *New York Times* article about schools refers to him, and he listed dates of visits with Yankee teachers in Jacksonville and Gainesville in his diary. His concern for their well-being in 1866 led him to reserve firewood to heat their classrooms. Swaim's activities in education predate the formulation of church policy—the content of which his correspondence with bishops may have helped to produce. On November 15, 1866, the bishops of the M.E. Church adopted a program of action. Freedom for African Americans came with the responsibility to educate them. Since southern states refused to perform this duty, the task fell to the church. Because "colored children are growing up in utter ignorance, Christian philanthropy must supply this lack. Religion and education alone can make freedom a blessing."[42] The bishops sought funds for the creation of schools across the South and linked the activities of teachers to those of missionaries. They claimed that "the school must be planted by the side of the church." To these the clerics added a call for action, "The emergency is upon us, and we must begin work now."[43]

While educational change was a vital part of Swaim's dream, so too was agricultural experimentation. At the end of the summer of 1866, Swaim purchased strawberry plants in New York, only to lose them in the shipping. Still other experiments required a larger plot, and in the fall he cleared land for farming. In the following May he harvested tomatoes and sent them to New York, realizing six dollars a bushel. He also said he produced "Irish potatoes, green beans and green corn in perfection by the last week in April." The success of these endeavors meant, he wrote, "that the general produce business" might outshine the profits that could be made from citrus.[44]

As John Swaim recorded the loss of his strawberries and the purchase of his farm in his diary for 1866, he also noted his friends and acquaintances. Harrison Reed appears in his diary on a dozen occasions between March 7 and June 14, and on this last day, the minister borrowed his horse. Reed had returned to Florida before Salmon Chase's visit. When the chief justice came in May 1865, it triggered a very negative response from the postal agent Reed. He wrote to the postmaster general to warn him that Chase sought "to secure this state for his future purposes."[45] Remembering his troubles with Lyman Stickney, Reed speculated that Chase's agents were already conducting "nefarious plans." The head of the postal service evidently bought this interpretation and passed the letter on to President Johnson, adding the comment that "these Chase vermin should be squelched."[46]

In the months that followed Chase's visit, the postal agent learned of Swaim's plans for Florida. The two men were together when the minister sought land for his farm in 1866. After some reflection, they both returned to a plot on Kings Road. Swaim wrote, "We were increasingly pleased with the appearance of the lots and concluded to take the whole tract."[47] When Reed returned to Jacksonville on March 24, 1866, both men watched the surveying of the land. The success of agricultural experiments interested the postal agent, and they remained a concern of his for coming decades.

Both men believed in the economic potential of modern Florida and the necessity of railroads to move produce and tourists. Yet they differed over the role of conservative leaders such as Governors Marvin and Walker and former Senator David Yulee. These politicians, like Reed, were closely connected to Andrew Johnson, and Yulee controlled the railroad that ran from Fernandina to Cedar Key, linking the Atlantic Ocean to a Gulf port. Always impressed with railroad executives, or potential millionaires, Reed sought Yulee's favor. The latter responded by suggesting that "they and their associates cooperate to rule the state, a plan which would preserve Florida's economic and social systems virtually intact while conceding certain protections and rights to blacks."[48] Swaim responded by questioning the likelihood of this arrangement, and both men agreed to disagree. There is humor in Swaim's articles, and they may have teased each other about their differences. The separate ground they stood on was quite distinctly divided: economic development with minimal social and political change versus economic development with major social and political change.

Early in Presidential Reconstruction it seemed that Reed was on target. As months passed, political discontent with Johnson's policies deepened in the North. Opposition grew and radicals campaigned vigorously against him. More in tune with public sentiments, radicals routed Democrats and Republicans loyal to the president in the 1866 elections. When the new Congress convened in 1867, radicals held more than enough seats to overturn the president's policies, pass their own agenda for the South, and override Johnson's vetoes. Yet at the end of Presidential Reconstruction, Reed held a stronger position than most of Johnson's allies. By efficiently reestablishing the postal service in Florida, he gained favor among some Republicans and Democrats. His position gave him unique advantages. He had the ability to influence the hiring of local postal agents, and his job came with free railroad passes, allowing him to travel widely. Thus, Reed rapidly became one of the better known Yankee strangers in the state. As he cultivated relationships around Florida, he also developed them with the business community in Jacksonville. He, like Swaim, came to know and value Calvin L. Robinson, a man who not only owned businesses and real estate investments but also forged important political connections. As a leader in the Unionist community, he earned the distinction of being Florida's first Republican national committeeman.[49]

While Harrison Reed, as postal agent, laid the foundation for a political future, Frederick Stowe joined his cousin, Christopher Spencer Foote, in Jacksonville in 1865. They rented Laurel Grove, a cotton plantation a few miles south of the town. Hiring local freedmen, they planted 200 acres of cotton. Just before the crop matured, "army worms," a larva that devours cotton, ate everything. Harriet Beecher Stowe wrote, "In two days our beautiful cotton field stood bare, without a leaf, as if a fire had passed over it."[50] From an investment of $10,000, the author's son produced two bales, doubtless some of the most expensive cotton ever raised.

Adding to this misfortune was Fred Stowe's inability to manage himself, let alone others. Wounded in the head at Gettysburg, he had developed headaches that aggravated his alcoholism. A family member claimed that after his injury the smallest amount of wine almost instantly made him drunk. Hypersensitivity to alcohol can be related to other drugs, and perhaps this was the case. Joan Hedrick in her 1994 biography of his mother notes that Harriet Beecher Stowe suffered from lead poisoning as a young adult. As a consequence, she bore five children before having a healthy and happy baby. Whatever the underlying reasons, Fred's behavior became a source of family concern and embarrassment, and Stowe willingly sent him to Florida. In doing so she reaped a financial disaster.[51]

While Fred was living at Laurel Grove, Ansel and Emma Kinne prepared to leave the state. Chloe Merrick was gone and so too would be the orphanage. In the summer of 1866, Osborn fired his own superintendent of public instruction. He then proposed to the NFRA that it combine its leadership with that of the Freedmen's Bureau. Rather than having two superintendents, there would be only one. Osborn expected Kinne to resign rather than accept a position under his leadership. Such plotting proved unnecessary since the Kinnes were exhausted, and their hopes for true freedom for African Americans under Presidential Reconstruction were dim. They left Florida at the end of the year to resume their lives in Syracuse.[52]

Presidential Reconstruction was a harrowing experience for many African Americans, costing them trusted friends and allies. Some Yankee strangers departed the South having struggled and given birth to a new social agenda. The Fernandina activists' initial euphoria of success was replaced by despair, while activists in Jacksonville prospered. It was in the latter area that the Stowes settled.

Early Congressional Reconstruction

Mandarin and Jacksonville

Charles Beecher and his famous sister sailed with Fred from Jacksonville to Laurel Grove. In his diary Charles recorded his stunning introduction to Florida: "There was a light breeze which tempered the heat. We had a supply of crackers and cheese and the skipper had a pie. It was the most beautiful picnic I ever enjoyed. The river stretched away so boundlessly on every hand [that] it seemed rather [like] a great sea or lake. The air was full of fragrance and the whole tropical scene was indescribably pleasing, far surpassing our summer excursions to the seashore." Later, as the wind faded away, they took turns rowing a boat. "I could not have conceived of an entrance to Florida life more to my taste."[1]

Harriet Beecher Stowe, fifty-five years of age, arrived in Jacksonville on March 10, 1867, with one of her favorite brothers and a head full of objectives. Beyond her need for a protected location for her son Fred, at a safe distance from vicious gossipers, she longed to escape from winter weather. Or, as she put it, "a place of refuge from the horrors which always make my life a burden."[2] Being in the South on the eve of Congressional Reconstruction also gave her an opportunity to participate in religious and social reform. Stowe confided to Charles: "My plan is not in any sense a mere worldly enterprise. I have for many years had a longing to be more immediately doing Christ's work on earth. My heart is with that poor people whose cause in words I have tried to plead and who now, ignorant and docile, are just in that formative stage in which whoever seizes them has them. Corrupt politicians are already beginning to speculate on them as possible capital for their schemes."[3]

As Stowe contemplated her involvement in reform, she turned to Charles, who had accompanied her on her European tour following the publication of *Uncle Tom's Cabin*. Her brother lived and worked in the South and had shared his knowledge with her, especially for *Uncle Tom's Cabin*. Besides giving her notes that led to the character Simon Legree, he had described the lavish lifestyles of wealthy planters in Louisiana and the plight of their slaves. After beginning *Uncle Tom's Cabin*, Mrs. Stowe had realized that she needed to consult her brother about the details of southern life. Writing him, she claimed "to be unable to do anything."[4] The answer to her problems, she insisted, lay in his instant help. Charles had responded quickly to her wishes, placing his pastorate in their father's hands. By having him accompany her on her Florida trip, she gained an ally who possessed firsthand insight and who was sympathetic to her objectives and actively concerned about her well-being.

Once in Jacksonville, Harriet and Charles visited local churches and toured African American schools. They seemed to Charles "equal [to] our schools of a similar grade." This visit to Jacksonville also gave him a chance to observe a black political rally. Beecher found the demeanor of African Americans to be very "earnest," and they "behaved better than [the participants of] any northern political meeting would have done."[5] In spite of the excesses of one of the speakers, the meeting provided "sublime" moments. Charles wrote, "Those at the North who think the freedmen do not want the suffrage or that they will be tools of their masters need only attend one such meeting to be cured of their delusion forever." Impressed by African Americans, Beecher observed in his diary, "They felt to the depths of their being all that suffrage implies. I must confess I never in my life realized what voting is, and is worth, as I did that night."[6]

While Stowe organized the house at Laurel Grove into a comfortable dwelling, unpacking luxurious amenities like carpets, china, and fine furniture, Charles explored the area. He helped Fred drag in an alligator that the younger man had shot, fished for bass, and rode around the farm.

Within a few days of arriving at the plantation, he sailed across the river, some four miles wide, to Mandarin. Charles wanted to purchase eggs and to see an orange grove. The trip left vivid impressions: "The orange trees were just done blooming and the oranges were visible about the size of a [rifle] shot. The air was delicious [and] the wild orange trees were full of oranges which are too sour for eating though used to some extent for lemonade. There are five acres, only about a fourth of it in trees, and a small house." Further down the shore was an even larger place for sale— one which had "fewer trees and more ground." Discussions with local people disclosed that one farmer sold 1500 dollars' worth of oranges in a single season. Intrigued, Charles wanted "to see as many of the plantations" as he could.[7]

Because his wife was not with him, Charles soon returned home to New England, while Stowe turned her attention from Laurel Grove and delayed her own departure. Sometime during her first visits to Florida, she became aware of John Swaim's vision. There were multiple avenues for this to have occurred. After she purchased land at Mandarin, Stowe and her family developed a close relationship with the Cranes, neighbors who lived just across a hedge. A daughter in this family became one of Mrs. Stowe's "favorites."[8] The famous author would call on them before breakfast. The Crane family came from Newark in 1865, where C. G. Crane had been an alderman. It is likely that they knew about Swaim's plans to seize Florida since articles in the *Newark Sentinel of Freedom* specifically mention the family at Mandarin.[9] Yet another avenue came from Fred's familial relationship with Christopher Spencer Foote, one of the partners in the Laurel Grove venture. Foote, Mrs. Stowe's nephew, traveled throughout the local countryside when Harrison Reed began his own farm in South Jacksonville, just a short distance away.

However it happened, Stowe, like Swaim, soon believed that "her Florida mission depended upon founding a colony." To that end, she wrote a prospective buyer of property in Mandarin, "we are very anxious for New England men to come among us. Ours is a sort of colony [where] six or eight young men have come in and are trying experiments in agriculture."[10] She added that, while progress continued, they still would "hail" every newcomer "from the North." Since potential recruits included family members, she turned to Charles and sought to entice him: "We are now thinking seriously of a place in Mandarin much more beautiful than any other in the vicinity. It has on it five large date palms, an olive tree in full bearing, besides a fine orange grove which this year will yield about 75,000 oranges. If we get that, then I want you to consider the expediency of buying the one next to it. It contains about two hundred acres of land, on which is a fine orange grove, the fruit from which last year brought in $2,000 at the wharf."[11]

Charles did not purchase the land in Mandarin, and Stowe changed her plans and bought the farm she originally had recommended to him. In doing this, she acted with an urgency that suggested not only a knowledge of changing land prices but also a mindset fitting Swaim's vision. In a letter to her husband, she wrote, "I want you to send [Spencer Foote] the $5000 [to pay for the farm] at once—either by selling any of our stock—or borrowing the money on our house. Only send it." Soon after this demand, she became the proud owner of an orange grove.[12]

Having made this purchase, she had the cottage on the property modified to meet the needs of her family and to accommodate grove manager Foote and his wife and child. They added a "wide veranda all round" the dwelling and constructed new rooms with steep gabled roofs, until, as Stowe said, it "was like nobody else's." The house stood so close to the trunk of an enormous live oak that it gave Mrs. Stowe the impression that the house was a part of the tree.

At this time, Stowe's career began to decline, and she worked to restore it by writing a book about New England village life, the life of her youth. Although she labored at great length over *Oldtown Folks*, it proved to be overly long and received poor reviews. Many women in the first half of the century had developed their writing skills by producing books to be read by families in parlors. Times, however, had changed; in the latter part of the century, one historian notes, "the reading public did not have the same leisure to bestow on books."[13] In addition, literary magazines began shaping public opinion, and they were dominated by men. *The Nation*, for instance, "insisted that the important issues of Reconstruction should be decided in the political arena" and that "literary women should give up their pulpits, pens, and podiums."[14] With constant attacks on their works, women found the environment of the 1870s to be a hostile one. Even so, Stowe fought back through a publicity campaign, and *Oldtown Folks* sold 25,000 copies between May and August of 1869.

Although she had hoped to improve her career, Stowe soon hurt her reputation by a damaging controversy that had implications for Florida. Biographer Joan Hedrick recounts, "On Stowe's second trip to England in 1856 she had become a confidant of Lady Byron, who had revealed to her the sordid sexual history of her estrangement from Lord Byron. Publicly, Lady Byron had maintained a stoic silence, believing it to be the best defense of true womanhood. Privately, she told Stowe the whole story, seeking her advice as to whether it might be better to break her silence."[15] Some years later Byron's lover published an account of the end of the marriage, depicting Byron's wife as at fault. Seeking to right this injustice, Stowe decided to share her knowledge of the story and to make the treatment of women the topic of public concern. While her exposé, *Lady Byron Vindicated*, faithfully portrayed Lady Byron's account of what happened, the story had problems. Byron's wife was dead and aspects of their marital relationship suggested that she had participated in a marriage of convenience. To this British newspapers added the probability that Lady Byron suffered, as the *London Times* put it, from a "delusion."

By raising the topic of the sexual exploitation of women, Stowe ventured into a subject that many did not want addressed. Newspapers and magazines seized upon the problems with Stowe's account and posed still more questions. If Lady Byron had behaved nobly, why would she have stayed married to her husband when he committed incest? How could such a woman really be as saintly as Stowe suggested? As the sordid debate continued and Stowe did not offer conclusive proof for her account, questions arose about Stowe's motives. As the *Independent* put it, "An authoress of reputation had [gotten] hold of a disgusting story about Byron—a story which, true or false, is revolting and obscene." She sold it to the press, who used the media to stimulate "the meanest curiosity of the public."[16] The consequences were, according to the newspaper, a financial "success" and a moral quagmire. According to many, Stowe failed to help Lady Byron's reputation and further damaged her own.[17]

After this episode, Stowe was less open in her defense of women. "Having gotten severely burned in this early attempt to speak of woman's wrongs," she, as Hedrick put it, "retreated to her earlier posture of speaking indirectly and attempting to wield her influence behind the scenes."[18] This decision emerged after the book's publication in January 1870, and early in her involvement in Florida. It seems that Stowe transferred this policy to her activities in the South. She publicly courted tourists and aggressively sought recruits for Yankee colonies without explaining the purpose of the settlements. While John Swaim, as a cleric with the support of his denomination, became secure enough to describe his agenda openly in newspapers, Stowe could achieve better results without doing so.[19] Motivating people to move to Florida would yield political and social consequences—a direct product of her activities. An open description of her goals would have damaged social objectives, Yankee efforts to seize a southern state. Moreover, it would no doubt have been publicly maligned in the wake of the Lady Byron episode.

Stowe dwelled at great length on the state's climate and beauty as well as its economic attractiveness. At other times, she described pleasant lawn parties and children chasing butterflies. She avoided publishing accounts of her relationships with prominent local Yankees. An example may be seen in her description of the Mitchells' lavish estate and gardens. The Mitchell home, the site of famous parties, stood on a point on the river between Mandarin and Jacksonville. Significantly, Stowe's article omits references to social gatherings or even the full identify of the estate's owner. Omissions by the editor, Harrison Reed, seem unlikely. Reed normally showed deference to important persons, whether traditional southerners or Yankees. Impressed by power, he was delighted to print an article by a famous writer. As a consequence, the article probably appears as Stowe wrote it—and it does not identify Mrs. Mitchell as Harrison Reed's wealthy sister, Martha Reed Mitchell.[20]

While the Byron incident plagued Harriet Beecher Stowe, Charles Beecher needed a respite from his own troubles. In 1867 he was still coping with the consequences of a heresy trial. Like other members of the family, he explored both spiritualism and transcendentalism. Ideas from both helped to confirm a belief that souls had multiple existences. Souls or spirits came to earth, according to Charles, for purification. Ultimately they could be reconciled to God. While such beliefs found acceptance among family members, they proved too daring for the religious community in northern Massachusetts. Some in Georgetown attacked these beliefs as evidence of heresy and tried to remove Charles from the pulpit. Since the Beechers challenged theological ideas, they had been tried for heresy on earlier occasions. What was new was that these opponents—"moles and bats," as Harriet Beecher Stowe called them—actually convicted him.[21] The decision threatened to divide Beecher's congregation and left him in the horrible situation of being labeled "unsound." Being a Beecher, Charles refused to flee. A vote by his congregation gave him support, and the congregation, in turn, charged the church conference with overstepping its authority. Although the church rescinded the heresy conviction, the entire incident dragged on for years, beginning before the battle of Gettysburg in 1863 and lingering into the summer of 1867. It ended after Charles returned home from his first Florida trip and offered to resign. His congregation supported him until the "bats" gave up.[22]

The tarnishing label of *heretic* came to a man who, like his half brother James, did not even want the ministry. Born in 1815, some eleven years before James, Charles Beecher displayed talent in poetry and music. His scholarly pursuits enabled him to graduate from college at nineteen, "near the top of his class." Disregarding the young man's preferences, his father, Lyman Beecher, steered him into the ministry, as he did all of his sons. Yet studying under his father at Lane Seminary did not create the desired result. Instead, Charles began questioning almost every aspect of Christian doctrine. Rather than going to sea, he fled to Louisiana to become a bill collector. In time, he recovered his faith, and in 1844 he became the pastor of a small Presbyterian church in Indiana. Beginning his ministry, he attacked the curriculum of important seminaries. As he put it, "They make it 'criminal' to 'say something new'. They make 'it shocking to utter words that have not the mold of age upon them'."[23] After this initial sermon, controversy followed him to Newark, where he campaigned on behalf of abolition. Then, in 1857, he moved to a Congregational church in Georgetown, where he was harassed for his beliefs.

Coming south in March 1867 with his sister Harriet offered a respite from these struggles. On the sea journey the weather along the New Jersey coast was very rough. While Stowe and the other passengers hid below deck, sick in their staterooms, Charles reveled in the violent storm. Reflecting the agony of his spirit, he wrote, "Sea rising. Driving before the gale I notice that though [we] are driven by storm and wind we are yet outstripped by the waves. Hour after hour I stood watching them chase us. A vast green roller and from ten to twenty feet high would come racing after us, reach us on our larboard quarter, pass under and off ahead—a magnificent pyramid of foaming emerald. As the wave came out from under the ship it would seem to exalt in having won the race, and would often leap up into a solid wave; bursting into foam and flashing away. I could not help exclaiming, 'Beautiful! O beautiful!'"[24]

Once in Florida, he found joy in the scenery. In his diary he wrote, "The nearer I get to nature the more composed my spirit [becomes]. It is a relief to be far, far removed from the competition, the strife, the press and the wearing responsibilities of our crowded New England life."[25] When he returned to New England, problems returned, and, while the heresy controversy soon ended, he was then battered by personal tragedy. Within approximately a year he lost three children. His son, who barely survived wounds at Gettysburg, died fighting Native Americans on the frontier, and two daughters drowned in a boating accident within sight of the family home. Returning to Florida in November 1869, Charles was ill in body and spirit. He wrote his wife, "How I long for home and you. I think constantly of you and of the dear children both living and dead. Elsie, Hattie, and Fred are ever with my thoughts and I have such longings to see them that I can hardly endure it. Every child, every girl, every young man I see that the least suggests a resemblance, fills me with emotions."[26]

Needing the healing tranquility of Florida, Beecher traveled to Mandarin, where he found that real estate prices had dramatically increased. Rather than investing his limited resources there, he went to Tallahassee and then to the largely abandoned village of Newport, some fourteen miles to the south. At Newport he found property at a fraction of the cost of land in Mandarin and a small farm that attracted him. He wrote his wife, "The house is one story, sixty-five feet long by thirty feet wide, with a porch in front. There is a hall thirteen by seventeen and a parlor on one side and a sitting room on the other. There are nine rooms in all. There is another building corner wise to this and nearly as large with a similar porch, containing five or six rooms for kitchen servants."[27] Beyond these structures stood a barn, outbuildings, and an orange grove. About a third of the 334 orange trees were sweet, suggesting that in a good season the farm could "pay for itself." When rail lines bypassed Newport, most of its residents moved away. Yet the prospect of having few neighbors did not bother Beecher. Whenever he wished, he could go to nearby St. Marks and catch trains for Tallahassee and Jacksonville. In a day or so he could be in Mandarin with his sister. Deciding to purchase the farm, Beecher resigned from his pastorate for reasons of health. Perhaps to his surprise, his congregation voted to give him a leave of absence.

The increases in real estate prices that propelled Beecher away from Mandarin fueled the hopes of Harriet Beecher Stowe and John Swaim. Prospering conditions offered greater attractions for northern immigrants. In 1867 Swaim could still describe land at "reasonable rates."[28] Yet early in 1869, he would say that "real estate in the city had doubled in value within [the last] twelve months."[29] By June he claimed that 260 buildings were under construction in Jacksonville at one time: "The town is growing with astonishing rapidity and carpenters were never more busy. Dwellings and stores are being erected in every nook and corner."[30]

The tourist trade grew and 14,000 winter visitors were reported in 1870. Among them were many residents from New Jersey. One writer in the *Sentinel of Freedom* found "no less than six Newarkers in the little village [of Green Cove Springs] at present."[31] Besides looking over the hotel register and finding many familiar names, he believed that Jersey men and women could be seen "at every point." To cope with a growing influx of tourists, northern investors built large hotels in Jacksonville in 1868. The St. James opened on January 1, 1869, with 120 rooms. A local historian observes, "Hot and cold baths were provided—an innovation in the day; there were bowling alleys and a billiard room for the amusement of guests."[32] Within twelve years additions to the hotel gave it another 400 rooms. The St. James soon found competition with other well-known establishments that were almost as large.

Dramatic changes in the tourist trade were accompanied by experiments in agriculture. In August 1868 Swaim reported that four Yankees planted early "tomatoes, watermelons, cucumbers, peas, and string beans."[33] Doing their own labor, they produced an extensive crop—some 75 bushels of tomatoes and 1,500 watermelons for the New York market: "The net proceeds of their sale were two thousand dollars for each man."[34] By 1868, Swaim believed that a "majority of the experiments made with raising early vegetables [were] quite satisfactory."[35] With the windfall from the tomato and melon sale, the four Northerners contemplated moving their families to Florida.

A different writer claimed in the *Sentinel of Freedom* that the state attracted three groups—those who were ill, often with consumption; those who sought "pleasure"; and those who "spied out the land for investment or occupancy."[36] While this third group brought capital, much of it went into speculation. Even so, the writer knew that "several farms are being cleared for orange groves and vegetable gardening." Most of the experimentation came from "northern enterprise and capital." It seemed that southern residents were too poor to risk their resources or were "too wedded to their old mode of doing things."

The same notions appeared in the *Boston Daily Advertiser*: "Of the new enterprises and new experiments in the State, nine-tenths are made by northern men, who form but an inconsiderable fraction of the whole population."[37] Its author believed that vegetables could be harvested three months earlier in Florida than in other places. As a consequence, tomatoes sent north in May sold for ten dollars a bushel in New York. Since the transportation cost only one dollar a bushel, the writer thought, "profits are fearful to estimate": "They propose to furnish the northern markets with green peas in March, Irish potatoes in April and May, melons in May and June and lettuce, radishes, cucumbers, turnips, etc., every month of the year."[38] In spite of the potential, which seemed to be transparent, there were those clinging to the past: "A planter came to the Ocklawaha River about fifteen years ago to make a cotton plantation. For this purpose he cleared five hundred acres and cut down and burned fifty thousand orange trees. If he had grafted them [to make the sour oranges sweet], at that time," he would be "a millionaire now."[39] Such a result was possible because the demand for oranges was so great and the supply so small that they seldom reached markets north of Charleston.

The realization of Swaim's goals required more than innovations in agriculture—it also needed the meaningful participation of African Americans. To that end, he continued assisting local schools, noting progress among black children. In 1868 he "ventured the opinion that there are as many colored boys and girls able to read fluently as can be found among the whites. If true (and I think it is) it speaks well for the capacity of the race—to achieve such a result in the brief season they have been allowed to receive instruction."[40] To further the cause of education, outreach was made to the Peabody fund. Its leaders promised to give the town $2,000 for a common school, if it raised $1,000. Swaim assured his readers that the "appropriation had already been made." With the combination of schooling, and jobs in bustling hotels and businesses, African Americans settled in the town of Jacksonville. A reporter claimed that wages were higher in urban areas and a "loftier style [of living] may be indulged."[41] As a result, the town and its suburbs claimed 6,187 residents—the majority of whom were black.

With the arrival of new immigrants, Swaim became confident about the future of modern Florida. He continued attracting tourists and in 1868 offered them a description of St. Augustine's historic buildings. At the same time he openly shared his dream and reacted in print to conservative southerners. With the beginning of Congressional Reconstruction, former Florida Governor Walker vented emotion. Referring to Congressional Reconstruction, he said that he would rather be with his "loved ones in honorable graves than live under the oppressive government."[42] Swaim responded by accusing Walker of not representing the majority of Floridians. The whole topic would become irrelevant if Yankees continued moving into the state. Swaim added, "The best way, and the only way to fix those fellows is to settle 'em out—settle 'em out! . . . . That's the way, settle them out. Come Kansas and Nebraska over them."[43]

To encourage the settlement of more Yankee strangers, John Swaim, not unlike Stowe, turned to family, his three sons. Jacob W. Swaim, the youngest, a bank clerk, moved to Jacksonville, arriving in 1867 with his wife and daughter. They were followed shortly by Thomas Sargent Swaim, a jeweler, and his wife and children. The third and last son, Matthias Freeman Swaim, an educator and Methodist Episcopal minister, arrived in the early 1870s. While idealism may have been a factor with all three men, their father accurately portrayed economic opportunities to them. They sought the bounty that this part of the South offered and found genuine success in their careers.[44]

Jacksonville became "an enterprising Yankee town in the South," or, as Republican Congressman William J. Purman described it, "a Northern city in a Southern latitude."[45] As this happened, northern Methodists moved their meeting place from a Presbyterian church to their own sanctuary. In February 1870 trustees were selected for Trinity Methodist Episcopal Church. Among them were John Swaim and Calvin Robinson—with the minister being selected as pastor. Church leaders purchased two lots and erected a small two-story sanctuary and parsonage. The church's interior was sparse, with evergreen branches rather than plaster covering the walls for Swaim's first sermons. Even so, the church gradually attracted local Yankees, and its location near the St. James Hotel was ideal for appealing to tourists. Within a decade or two it became the largest northern Methodist church in Florida. Committed to his agenda and to his vision of racial cooperation, Swaim responded to the needs of African Americans long before those of Yankee strangers. The construction of a black church, Zion M.E., predated Trinity by almost four years.[46]

In 1870 Jacksonville and Mandarin were becoming places altogether different from those seen by James and Frankie Beecher in 1864. Soon Yankees and visitors from "all over the world" promenaded through Jacksonville's main shopping district. As one historian notes, "The bazaars, curio shops, and stores which lined Bay Street were thronged with well-dressed people on pleasure bent. Representatives of the New York and London society clubs, money kings, literary celebrities, dowagers and their daughters, bridal couples and Bohemians jostled one another in their round of pleasure."[47] The social experiment of the Beechers, Stowes, Swaims, Reeds, and others turned into reality. Before this happened, however, reformers used state government to change Florida.

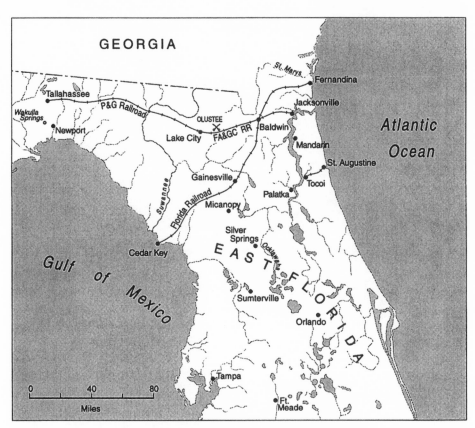

Florida in the Reconstruction period. Courtesy of Canter Brown.

Harriet Beecher Stowe, 1811–1896. Prints and Photographs Division, Library of Congress, Washington, D.C.

Chloe Merrick Reed, 1832–
1897. By permission of the
State Historical Society of
Wisconsin, Madison. Negative
no. WHI(X3)35125.

Chloe Merrick's multiracial orphanage in Fernandina. Courtesy of the U.S. Army Military History Institute, Carlisle.

Harrison Reed, 1813–1899. By permission of the State Historical Society of Wisconsin, Madison. Negative no. WHI(x3)26093.

James C. Beecher, 1828–1886. By permission of the Harriet Beecher Stowe Center, Hartford, Connecticut.

Union troops on parade during their occupation of Fernandina. Courtesy of the Florida Photographic Collection, Florida State Archives, Tallahassee.

Charles Beecher, 1815–1900. By permission of the Harriet Beecher
Stowe Center, Hartford, Connecticut.

The Stowe family at home in Mandarin—a sight tourists always hoped to see. Courtesy of the Florida Photographic Collection, Florida State Archives, Tallahassee.

Villa Alexandria, the home of Martha Reed Mitchell, was described by Harriet Beecher Stowe as a "terrestrial paradise." Courtesy of the Florida Photographic Collection, Florida State Archives, Tallahassee.

Cookman Institute, Jacksonville, Florida (later Bethune-Cookman College, relocated to Daytona Beach). Courtesy of the Florida Photographic Collection, Florida State Archives, Tallahassee.

Chloe Merrick Reed in 1893. Courtesy of the Florida Photographic Collection, Florida State Archives, Tallahassee.

Harrison Reed

Politics and Marriage

The course of reform in Florida depended upon national and state politics. Both came together to bring Harrison Reed to the governor's office. Once he was there, circumstances drove him away from his conservative inclinations. Shortly before Harriet Beecher Stowe and her brother left New York on March 6, 1867, for their first trip to Florida, a new Congress convened. The elections of the preceding fall had transferred enormous power to radical Republicans. Under the leadership of radicals like Charles Sumner and Thaddeus Stevens, Congress passed the First Reconstruction Act on March 2, 1867. This legislation suspended state governments in every southern state except Tennessee, creating five military districts. In the legislation that followed the First Reconstruction Act, Congress outlined a formula for the South. It disbarred former leaders of the Confederacy from public office and required conventions to draft new state constitutions. Congress demanded suffrage for African Americans to be an integral part of political life, and it required the states to ratify the Fourteenth Amendment and hold new elections. These events transformed politics in Florida as in other parts of the South and accelerated the formation of the state's Republican Party.[1]

In 1867 Harrison Reed continued expanding his network of political friends and sought to strengthen his alliance with traditional southern leaders such as David Levy Yulee and soon-to-be-ousted Governor Walker. In exchange for their support, Yulee wanted Reed's help in forming a Conservative Party as an alternative to the Republican Party in

Florida. While it could be largely Republican in character and it could send Unionists and Yankees to public offices, Yulee and Walker wanted the party to be "independent" and have a name other than *Republican* or *Radical*. Reed, who had links to nominal Republicans in Washington, accepted this proposal and set out to further Yulee's goals through the Union Republican Club of Jacksonville—a political organizing body that had been formed in the office of Unionist lawyer Ossian B. Hart on April 4, 1867. Its members included Reed's friends, Unionist allies of Hart, Calvin Robinson, and John Swaim. In spite of the postal agent's efforts, the Yulee proposal was recognized as an effort to preserve the "political influence and economic power of the [former] Rebel leadership."[2] Such a notion brought vigorous opposition from Hart, who successfully fought Reed's plans.

While this disagreement raged and threatened to divide Republicans in Jacksonville, other groups formed. The most radical was led by two white Yankees, Liberty Billings and Daniel Richards, and an African American from Maryland, William U. Saunders. According to historians these men formed Union League chapters wherever concentrations of freedmen could be found. The Union League appealed to African Americans by combining ritual and emotion with a philosophy that rejected social distinctions based upon race. The Florida leadership added ability to the pursuit of the league's racial objectives. Billings gave the group political insight. Saunders provided magnetic public speaking, and Richards had connections with the Washington congressional committee helping to organize the Republican Party in the South. Richards, in other words, had a ready access to funding.[3]

At the other end of the Republican spectrum stood Thomas W. Osborn and his allies. Osborn, after his service as head of the Freedmen's Bureau, stayed in Florida and organized a secret organization known as the Lincoln Brotherhood. This group included white leaders and important African American Baptist ministers who lived in plantation country from fifty miles east of Tallahassee to seventy or eighty miles west. Osborn's faction tended to be more conservative since many of its religious leaders preferred "peaceful accommodation with whites."[4]

In addition to these groups and the conservative businessmen and professionals associated with Reed in Jacksonville were Florida's Unionists. These men, some two or three thousand in number, greatly outnumbered the politically active Yankees by perhaps four to one. Their leader, Ossian Hart, was a native-born southerner and former Whig. In spite of his background, Hart sought more radical reforms than either Reed or Osborn. His preference for political and social change actually outstripped the wishes of many members of the Jacksonville business community. Hart's "mulish tenacity" for reform, as Reed put it, helped undercut the Unionists in 1867.[5] It may also have been a factor in Reed's growing influence in the town since he was more in tune with the sentiments of persons holding economic power.

Beyond these groups existed another important and ever-growing faction: the clergymen and lay leaders of the African Methodist Episcopal (AME) Church. This denomination's presence was new in Florida as of 1865. The church regarded the state as a priority at the end of the conflict and sent a very gifted person, Charles H. Pearce, to be its presiding elder. The AME church was perhaps the most vocal black church in political affairs, and Pearce endorsed the church's militant stance. He declared, "A man in this state cannot do his whole duty as a minister except [when] he looks out for the political interests of his people."[6] To further efforts in Florida, the church brought ministers from other places. Among these newcomers were both William G. Stewart and William Bradwell.

As the AME grew rapidly, it also welcomed into its ranks the pastors of existing local congregations who were not affiliated with other church bodies. This practice brought the AME a number of important ministers, especially Robert Meacham and Henry Call. Meacham, who had founded a church in Tallahassee, was sent to lead missionary efforts in nearby Jefferson County. A historian notes, "Henry Call similarly brought Florida contacts and experience to AME work in West Florida."[7] Additional strength came to the AME from its organizational structure. With a group of hierarchical positions ranging from lay leaders to ordained clergy to district officers, or presiding elders, it could coordinate its efforts and impose discipline among its members. While this simple bureaucratic structure helped to make the AME better organized than most of its rivals, such an advantage did not keep its leaders from being wary of other religious groups. Pearce was particularly concerned about the Baptists and their Lincoln Brotherhood.[8]

Rather than working cooperatively, as Swaim and Hart had assumed Republicans would, the various groups began to compete. Soon a pattern emerged, though the participants may not have realized it. Weaker factions joined together to block the group with the most power. Since the Unionists were the most numerous among white Republicans and they were local citizens with a native-born leader, an early agenda became stopping Ossian Hart. This goal was accomplished at the first party convention, in July 1867, when Osborn, backed by other factions, became the party chairman. Having victoriously outmaneuvered Hart, Billings personally attacked him: "A southern man could not be trusted, because a man born and brought up under old southern institutions and tainted with the evil influences of slavery could never understand as clearly, and carry out as effectively the true principles of liberty and equality as could men reared in a free atmosphere accustomed to free institutions."[9] These inflammatory words added to the defeat, with Hart hastily departing the convention.

Having blocked a popular local leader, the rest of the factions united to stop the radical team of Billings, Saunders, and Richards. As the time approached for the convention to draft a new state constitution, the radicals elected a majority of delegates based upon their call for social and political equality. As this majority became apparent, Osborn and Reed did their best to derail them. Postal agent Reed appealed to the military governor in Atlanta, seeking to keep nonresidents of Florida from the meeting. Reed noted that "William U. Saunders [was] a colored citizen of Maryland, Liberty Billings, a white citizen of New Hampshire, and Daniel Richards, a white citizen of Illinois."[10] When General Pope refused to help Reed, the postal agent went to his friends in Washington, D.C. They, in turn, cut off the funding for the radicals and transferred the monies to Reed.

When the convention met early in 1868, the radicals still held a majority of the delegates, and the other factions worked for a delay. Reed and Osborn appealed to former Rebels and, in the end, went to Ossian Hart to save Florida. They did this by getting enough delegates to withdraw from the convention, denying the radicals a quorum. When the meeting resumed on February 10, three African Americans switched their allegiance from the radicals to other factions. This enabled Osborn, Hart, and Reed to seize the convention, install new officers, and write a constitution. Rather than accepting defeat, the radicals publicly campaigned against the constitution and named their own candidates for state office. A historian continues, "The regular party organization named its candidates as well. Reed led the ticket for governor, with fellow Wisconsinite William H. Gleason for lieutenant governor."[11] As the May election approached, the radical ticket fractured, with candidates withdrawing or switching their allegiance to Reed.

The election ended without surprise and Reed became the state's chief executive. The rest of the Republican Party did very well, capturing two-thirds of the state senate and 37 of 53 seats in the assembly, or house of representatives. Since the military governor delayed transferring power until July 4, the legislature met first and approved the Thirteenth and Fourteenth Amendments to the U.S. Constitution. From these actions they moved on to the contest between Osborn and Hart for the U.S. Senate seat. In spite of help from the AME, Hart was again defeated, and Osborn claimed the position, giving him access to both patronage and federal funds.[12]

For the very special occasion of his inauguration, Reed invited intimate friends, including the Swaim family. The minister's son Jacob responded to the honor by describing it for the *Sentinel of Freedom*: "The colored population was fully represented in the crowds collected on the streets." At the same time, however, "very few of the native whites were to be seen, as they wish to utterly ignore the celebration of July Fourth."[13] Those opposed to change would not observe the holiday "and did not countenance the reconstruction of the State." Yet, in spite of their wishes, the transfer of power went on in an orderly fashion: "The Colonel commanding [John T. Sprague] and the Governor had a program to carry out, and the exercises were commenced at noon by a meeting in the Governor's room in the Capitol." At this time, "the necessary papers were exchanged, and then they walked, arm in arm, up to the Assembly room, followed by the [military] staff in full dress, the band playing 'Hail to the Chief'."[14] As they entered the room, they found that the senate had joined the lower house in a joint session. Then, according to Jacob Swaim, the colonel "made a brilliant speech alluding in a feeling and delicate manner to the friendly relations existing between himself and the Governor." Reed, in turn, responded with "appropriate words, acknowledging how much we were indebted to the mild course of military rule."[15] It was one of the more pleasant moments of Reed's life—he had translated his search for power and wealth into the governorship of a state.

With Yulee still in mind, Reed continued to court the state's traditional conservative leaders. To that end, he picked a number of Democrats for important offices. A historian notes, "Three of the seven circuit judges he placed on the bench were white conservatives, as was Comptroller Robert H. Gamble. For attorney general Reed turned to James D. Westcott, Jr., who had been closely linked to Florida's Confederate government."[16] Furthermore, Reed did not implement his promise to place an African American in the cabinet. He toyed with nominating the very able Jonathan C. Gibbs, a Presbyterian minister educated at Dartmouth and Princeton, as secretary of state, only to withdraw the recommendation. African Americans did receive numerous appointments but these were minor local ones. Further disappointments came when Reed vetoed laws that sought to protect civil rights and to organize a state public school system. The latter topic did not disappear, however, and the governor sent his state superintendent for public instruction on a tour to other states to learn about their efforts in drafting legislation.

The new constitution reflected the priorities of individuals such as John Swaim and Harriet Beecher Stowe by calling for a cabinet position of commissioner of immigration. To Reed's credit, he promptly filled the post with a competent person, New England–born J. S. Adams. Adams's job was, according to law, to "encourage the coming of new settlers."[17] Attracting Yankee residents was an objective that Reed also identified in addresses to the legislature. To him it was of the "highest importance to the present and future prospects of the state."[18] To that end, he encouraged Adams to write pamphlets praising its many advantages. The commissioner evidently took this task very seriously, and within three years Reed noted that the population of Florida grew by 40,000 new citizens. Adams, the governor felt, produced the result with publishing efforts and his "vast and widely-distributed correspondence."[19] Reed transformed John Swaim's efforts in publicizing Florida into an important state office. With Adams's success, Swaim's letters to the northern press became less frequent.

As governor, Reed learned the drastic extent of the state's poor financial condition. Florida spent funds faster than it collected them. A historian notes the state had "bonded debt and unpaid warrants that were reported at $644,607 in the fall of 1868. Large amounts of interest were due and unpaid. The revenue system was inefficient, and there was a large deficiency in the accounts of collectors."[20] To cover part of its obligations, the state issued scrip that traded at discounts, undercutting value. All of this created headaches for Reed, weakened his position, and left him at a disadvantage in dealing with leaders such as Osborn. Becoming a U.S. senator, Osborn gained, on the other hand, access to hard currency and to federal patronage for his political friends. The senator's support for the governor was very brief, and, when he realized that Reed wanted to exercise authority, he set out to get rid of him.

Reed assumed that when the legislature sought a special session in the fall of 1868 there could be mischief. Osborn's friends prepared and pressed a secret agenda. Suspicious, the governor limited the proclamation for the session. Reed instructed the legislature to select presidential electors. Rather than just following the governor's wishes, the state senate met "without a constitutional quorum."[21] As newspapers reported the drama, the Osborn faction then went to the house "and demanded the impeachment of the governor."[22] The house "promptly declared the governor impeached for high crimes and misdemeanors, and notified

Lieutenant Governor Gleason to assume Reed's office."[23] In this farce, the secretary of state went to Gleason's support, and the legislature, having done Osborn's bidding, adjourned.

Realizing the weakness of his position, Reed needed dramatic support and recognized that his conservative friends would not bring it to bear. With few options Reed turned to AME elder and state senator Charles H. Pearce. Meeting with Pearce, the governor "insisted that he had seen the error of his own ways."[24] The black leader, realizing that Osborn and his Baptist friends were seizing state government, reacted positively. In addition, Pearce, according to one African American senator, "became convinced that the Governor was sincere in trying to administer the government with honesty." Affirmation of Reed's character also came from John Swaim to readers in Newark. The Yankee minister found him, after four years of friendship, to be "a gentleman of sterling integrity, indomitable perseverance and good executive ability."[25] Even in recent decades Reed's efforts have received positive comments from historians knowledgeable about Reconstruction. Few have ever attributed the same merit to Thomas Osborn and his political friends—people Charles Beecher later found to be "odious."[26] For some, the bitter contest between the governor and senator was very basic; it was a contest between a semblance of responsible government versus none.

Reed reacted to the house's impeachment ruling by posting guards at the capital building, preventing Lieutenant Governor Gleason from occupying it. Then Reed removed the secretary of state from office, giving the position to Jonathan C. Gibbs. This decision offered tangible evidence that the promises made to Pearce were real, eliciting further African American support. Having made this bold move, placing a prominent and respected African American in his cabinet, Reed then turned to the state supreme court, seeking a ruling on the legality of the legislative session attempting to impeach him. The response, historians note, came quickly: "About two weeks later the justices returned their answers, unanimously sustaining the governor, holding in effect that there had been no legal legislature in extraordinary session."[27] Supporting the decision was Chief Justice Edwin W. Randall, brother to the postmaster general, and Ossian B. Hart, destined to be the next governor. Seeking to add to his victory, the governor sought to eliminate Gleason. Reed pointed out to the high court that the lieutenant governor had violated the state's residency laws, just as had Billings, Saunders, and Richards. The justices responded by issuing a "judgment ousting Gleason from office."[28]

These bold actions astonished the governor's opponents, generated support from African Americans, and won Reed respect where it counted the most. He outmaneuvered Osborn and his cronies, actions that pleased Chloe Merrick, who knew Reed from earlier days in Fernandina. Obviously still communicating with each other, Reed visited her at her new assignment in New Bern, North Carolina. After illness and the closing of the orphanage, she had accepted positions away from Florida— still committed to the education of freedmen. Reed went to Chloe Merrick and proposed to her. At least one scholar believes that "only the dignity of the governorship would have emboldened Reed to propose mar- riage."[29] A shift in his administration from the coddling of rebels to social activism could be seen in the Gibbs appointment. To further gain Merrick's favorable opinion, the governor hired her nephew, Charles Wesley Kinne, Ansel Kinne's son, as his personal secretary. To the same end, Reed developed a friendship with Chloe's Civil War admirer Milton Littlefield. The former Union officer, turned railroad speculator, renewed his own relationship with Merrick. Perhaps Reed believed Littlefield might exert a positive influence on his behalf.[30]

Reed's success at winning a governorship had been positive in Mer- rick's eyes, but his conservative, limiting decisions had not been. News of the later and sudden change came to Merrick as she struggled to "complete her life's work." At the time, the troubles of the National Freedmen's Relief Association (NFRA) continued to grow, and little could be done to prevent it from unraveling. Marriage to Harrison Reed would provide other avenues to her goals. With ideas fueled by growing up in an abolitionist family and social climate, she held expectations that went beyond those of many women of the day. As first lady she would have access to those in power, and Reed could help her with her agenda as he did in 1863. The governor confirmed this thought when the state superintendent for public instruction called upon her, seeking input for crafting school legislation.

Chloe Merrick and Harrison Reed were married at the Kinnes' Syracuse home on August 10, 1869.[31] One of the town's newspapers reported that the "ceremony was performed in the pleasant grove on Mr. Kinne's premises, by the Rev. Samuel J. May, in the presence of a small party of friends and family of the bride."[32] Suffragists of this era were already modifying marriage vows, and Chloe dropped any promise to "obey" her husband. Harrison, almost twenty years her senior, was in love and would have done whatever she wished.

The newlyweds traveled to Niagara Falls and then on to Reed's sister's home in Wisconsin. In Milwaukee relatives treated the couple as honored guests and held a reception. The newspaper Reed had led decades earlier reported that "quite a number of old citizens of Milwaukee gathered at the elegant and hospitable mansion of Alexander Mitchell last evening, to pay their respects to his brother-in-law, Governor Harrison Reed, of Florida, and his beautiful and estimable bride."[33] This event led to reflections on an earlier time when the city had been a village and Reed had struggled to organize the *Milwaukee Sentinel.* An evening of conversation and music ended with a congratulatory address, which noted that Reed "labored with industry and perseverance" at the newspaper and that he had shown the same characteristics in his personal life. While his old friends recognized the prejudice he faced in Florida, they hoped that the "virtues of temperance, truth, and justice" that he had shown in Wisconsin would win support in Florida. People in the North wanted to assure the residents in the South that they were led by a "respected citizen of Wisconsin."[34]

Reed, according to a reporter, responded to these compliments with the "quiet dignity and modesty that have ever characterized him."[35] He talked about the progress of Reconstruction in Florida, while stressing the potential for developing the state's resources. As he spoke, he stood in the extraordinary home of a man he truly admired. Alexander Mitchell had used his position as a director of the Milwaukee and St. Paul Railway Company to save the railroad from bankruptcy. Believing that "with proper management" the line "could be made to pay its way," Mitchell had accepted the challenge to take the company presidency in 1864. Within a year the line produced a profit. At the time, it was only several hundred miles long. "When Mitchell died in 1887," a writer reported, "Chicago, Milwaukee and St. Paul Railway Company owned and operated over 5,000 miles of railway, covering Wisconsin, northern Illinois, Minnesota, Iowa, and South Dakota."[36]

Alexander Mitchell's ties to Florida began before the onset of military Reconstruction and came through his wife, Martha Reed Mitchell, who was Governor Reed's sister. With her immense wealth, she arrived in Jacksonville in 1867 and purchased land on a point on the St. Johns River six miles north of Mandarin. In a rural area with impoverished residents, Mitchell built an unusual home, Villa Alexandria. It combined modest size with extraordinary quality. One guest thought "the dining room was a masterpiece of magnificence." Mahogany cabinets, said to have cost $50,000, lined its walls. Behind their glass doors she saw Mitchell's "marvelous collection of teapots from all over the world, patiently collected on her many trips abroad." The location of the dining room table changed, according to the number of her quests. If these were few in number, it would be moved into a bay window looking out upon the river. When guests entered the room, they found "fine paintings by European masters." While the dining room was extraordinary, Mrs. Mitchell's bedroom is said to have rivaled it in quality. Her bay window had white silk curtains surmounted with "blue brocade over-drapes." To enter the room, one had to walk up several steps, which, according to a guest, seemed to "lead up to her throne."[37] Once inside the room, visitors could see that the walls were decorated with "hand-carved" woodwork: "It was reported she had secured these carvings in France, had them carefully taken down and brought over and installed in her room."[38]

Harrison Reed admired the opulence, although he could not afford to emulate it. At Villa Alexandria he saw a French bedroom with "dainty blue and gold finished white antique furniture." Another frequent guest preferred the Japanese bedroom, "with heavy dark lacquered furniture." Corresponding with these rooms were baths. Martha's grandson David Mitchell believed that these were the first modern bathrooms served with plumbing south of Charleston: "She brought down expert builders and mechanics, so that every item was properly taken care of." Still another local resident recalled David's own bathroom, with "Tiffany glass windows, a bathtub carved out of a solid block of marble, the fittings mounted with ivory and silver. The large washstand also was of the same beautiful marble." When these did not suit David, he took showers or a Turkish bath in an adjoining "square bathing pool."[39]

The theme of refined elegance continued in the library. In it was a box, guests remember, containing "priceless" pictures on parchment of the "Holy Script—each being done by one of the old masters."[40] When Harrison Reed wandered into his sister's garden, he found plants from all over the world. A walk through these led to the boathouse, which had two levels. The upper room contained the Mitchell ballroom and "magnificent lounges for both men and women."[41] Provisions were made for serving guests iced drinks or imported liquors. Yet Reed no doubt remembered when the Mitchells had been newlyweds and had lived in a tiny cottage. All of the wealth that produced this earthly paradise had been earned by a couple, both of whom were, in fact, younger than himself. They had found fantastic wealth in Wisconsin. Reed had missed his opportunity in the North, but he was determined not to let his chances in Florida slip away.

Chloe Merrick Reed valued Mrs. Mitchell's home and in the future gave even stronger approval to her sister-in-law's generous support of charity. In 1869, however, Merrick focused upon her own agenda. Without a state-owned mansion in Tallahassee, the Reeds obtained a house on the west side of the capital building. As one might expect, she ran this dwelling with Yankee efficiency and neatness. William Constantine Beecher, nephew of Charles Beecher, visiting Florida in 1871, described the Reeds' residence as "one of the only pretty home like houses I saw."[42] People in the twentieth century still remembered it as the site of multiracial social gatherings. Such "scandalous behavior" actually began before their marriage, when Reed held a champagne party in the state capital to note Osborn's humiliating defeat.[43]

The Tallahassee social world that Chloe entered was not as rigid as many opposed to Reconstruction would have preferred. One very prominent family owned an important plantation just a few miles from the capital. Rather than excluding any political faction, the Hopkins family invited to social events Yankees and former Rebels alike. Interestingly, it seems that the most diverse and potentially unlikely guests would come and mix socially. This included not only the Reeds but also the person who would become the queen bee of local aristocrats, Susan Bradford Eppes. Whatever people felt about the Reeds, they had power and they had access to the army band. Or as Eppes put it, "The Regimental Band comes out often to play for us to dance, it makes fine music and we enjoy it."[44] The Hopkins family responded to the musicians by setting out "a large tray of refreshments" and sending flowers upstairs "to be thrown down to them."[45] According to her memoirs, Eppes drew the line at showering a Yankee band with roses and let the other women throw them.

Chloe Merrick Reed and the southern princess engaged in an amusing contest. Since the Hopkins home sheltered both Union officers and former Rebel leaders, one of the children, Arvah, was fascinated by uniforms. Susan made for him "a Confederate captain's uniform" with "brass buttons and gold lace." Since Union officers teased Arvah, making fun of him for being a Johnnie Reb, Chloe made him a Yankee uniform. She was a "neat hand at work and by night the little suit was finished and Arvah was the center of an admiring group."[46] The real fun came in getting the child to select the uniform to wear. For a while when Arvah wore blue, Susan Eppes withheld affection, saying that she could not love a Yankee. When this approach became ineffective, she resorted to paying him: "I took to slipping [him] a piece of money in his hand when it was time to dress for the evening and then, in spite of Mrs. Reed's pleading, he would wear the suit of gray." Yet when she forgot or didn't have a coin, "Arvah appeared in the parlor, a tiny figure in blue, where he was surrounded by

his brother officers and, listened with willing ears to the many complimentary speeches made for his benefit."[47]

Such diversions did not distract Chloe Merrick Reed from social reform. By the end of 1869, activists had a powerful and determined leader
in the governor's wife. She seized the opportunity, and Charles Beecher
would soon be appointed to her husband's cabinet.

Political Apex

Charles Beecher in Office

In spite of the many challenging complications in their lives, neither Harriet Beecher Stowe nor Chloe Merrick Reed ever lost sight of social reform. Before coming to Florida, the famous author expressed concern for the well-being of African Americans, an interest that continued in her annual visits to Mandarin. The state's needs seemed immense to her. In May 1870 she knew of "hundreds of miles" where a "scattered population lived without churches, schools, or means of improvement."[1] The situation at Mandarin was better. A school had been built with the help of the Freedmen's Bureau in 1869, adding to the dozen or so houses. This new building also doubled as a church, where her husband, Calvin, held services during the winter. Harriet Beecher Stowe illustrated the need for both churches and pastors, claiming that his efforts with the gospel were the only ones within fifteen miles. While it was accurate, she noted, that "young enterprising men from the Northern states" cleared land for citrus groves and agricultural experiments, they had to concentrate their limited resources on getting their farms into production. It would be unfair, according to her, to "expect them to support a minister" when they "can hardly support themselves."[2]

In preparation for his ministry at Mandarin, Calvin Stowe began very much as Merrick had in Fernandina. The professor, his wife wrote, "visited, on foot, all the families for a circuit of about seven miles around, entering into every house and forming the acquaintance of the inhabitants."[3] On these journeys he found a settlement of some fifty black families and perhaps a dozen homes owned by whites. The residents greeted him warmly; he "found a simple people, gratified with his visit, ready and pleased to enter into conversation." On one of these trips, he discovered a family that had lost a small child. The family, the professor learned, had buried the infant without a funeral or a minister to comfort the distraught mother. In an effort to help, the Stowes and other neighbors went to the child's home and offered both the singing of hymns and the reading of scripture.[4]

While Harriet Beecher Stowe sought ministerial help for Florida in the press, the family disseminated the faith. When an Episcopal missionary visited Mandarin for Easter 1870, professor Stowe notified families for miles around. His wife wrote, "The communion was administered in the Episcopal form by a clergyman from New York to a small band of different denominations. The majority were Episcopalians, but Baptists and Methodists and Congregationalists were there also, some black and some white, who knelt together at the altar."[5] It suited her purposes to note the willing participation of an African American patriarch and a woman who had missed communion for nine years. Other local Yankees went unmentioned, including Martha Mitchell, Chloe Merrick, and Harrison Reed.

However it happened, whether it was at Easter or later in 1870, Harriet Beecher Stowe and Chloe Merrick Reed met, for the author came to Chloe's assistance. When Florida's first lady arrived in Tallahassee, she found that a basic school law had been enacted by the legislature and signed by her husband. This legislation created school districts based upon the state's counties. It gave each county a school superintendent and a school board composed of five members: "All of the superintendents were to be appointed by the governor. They, in turn, nominated school board members for state approval."[6] This system eliminated the creation of smaller school districts, including ones based on towns and cities. Florida's current school system is a modification of this structure, with the school board positions having been changed from appointed to locally elected. The 1869 legislation also mandated a system of ad valorem taxes to pay for public education.

While this educational system was easily adapted to local needs, Democrats during Reed's time described it as a pyramid with a "dictator." Harrison Reed, however, was in a constant struggle with either the state's inadequate finances or with Osborn's political machine. As a consequence, the governor delegated these powers to the state superintendent of public instruction, Charles Thurston Chase. The results of this delegation became progressively less satisfactory. Education was a major goal of many African Americans, especially among Reed's friends in the African Methodist Episcopal (AME) Church, and they expected the administration to deliver. By marrying Chloe Merrick, with her own reputation among blacks, Reed added to their expectations. The first lady strengthened the governor's alliances with African Americans, which helped to keep him in office, and she shared goals similar to theirs. Even though one early historian described Chase as a "valuable public servant," his health deteriorated.[7] His absenteeism from work increased as he sought medical care out of the state. As months passed, Reed became impatient and began to publicly criticize the superintendent, hoping he would voluntarily resign. This proved unnecessary when Chase died on September 22, 1870.

Even though the governor gave thought to selecting a replacement, the position remained open for a time after the superintendent died. The number of potential candidates was actually small; the new superintendent needed to combine a knowledge of education with the ability to work closely with a creative and energetic woman. In the fall of 1870, Charles Beecher emerged as a candidate but resisted. It took until March 1871 before he was "induced by the Governor to accept the office," a change of heart that at least one historian believes was brought about by his sister.[8] Both Harriet Beecher Stowe and Chloe Merrick Reed shared an abiding commitment to high-quality education, and a conversation between them would have included the topic. The author valued Merrick's objectives, and the younger woman—with her abolitionist background, sense of humor, and record of Christian service—was a convincing advocate. On March 18, 1871, Charles Beecher joined the Reed administration, having been, as he wrote to the head of the Freedmen's Bureau, "almost coerced."[9]

During the time between the decision to move to Newport in 1869 and his acceptance of public office, Beecher lived quietly. As his physical and psychological health mended in the serene beauty, he preached among African Americans. His initial success soon faded. "I should have done them more good," he wrote, "but they heard that I 'was not sound'."[10] The heresy mess from an earlier period in his life dogged him even in his ministerial outreach in the South.

When Beecher became superintendent, he found the office in disarray. As Chase's health had deteriorated, everything had been neglected. A newspaper reported that there were "no records of transactions of the department" for 1870, and "the papers and correspondence in the office were in inextricable confusion."[11] Since Chase had been in office for three and one-half years, hundreds of documents had accumulated. Chase had replaced Ansel Kinne. In 1867 the National Freedmen's Relief Association and the Freedmen's Bureau had implemented Thomas Osborn's wishes and unified their separate leadership positions under the bureau. When the constitution of 1868 took effect and Reed began his administration, the governor appointed Chase to his last job. As one historian observes, "The connection between the Freedmen's Bureau and state government reflects the origins of Florida's current public school system."[12] When Chase started working for the bureau, only two kinds of schools existed: "The first had been established and supported by freedmen's aid societies, and the second had been established by private individuals seeking aid from the government."[13] Prewar schools, given an absence of public funding, were small and private. After years of conflict and disruption, these institutions disappeared.

Under Chase's supervision Freedmen's Bureau schools were organized with a set of guidelines. The bureau gave federal monies to communities to purchase building supplies—"lumber, nails, and shingles." It made these funds available to local school committees after these groups obtained clear title to a plot of land and pledges of money and labor to erect a building. While this policy helped to create a nucleus for Florida's public school system, major problems remained. Harriet Beecher Stowe found the state's population to be both sparse and scattered. When Chase took office, historians believe, there were shortages of every kind—"of school funds, a lack of administrative organization, an almost total lack of suitable buildings, textbooks, and supplies, a small and poorly trained teaching force, no clearly defined course of study, no provision for secondary or higher education, and no suitable school law."[14] African Americans supported public education, and Congressional Reconstruction enabled a majority of Floridians to express their desire for a public school system. This fact helps to explain the continuing growth in the number of schools after the beginning of the Reed administration. By Chase's death there were 250 schools and some 7,500 students.[15]

As Reed left public education to Chase, he then let his wife and Charles Beecher shape it. A later historian describes the government's achievements as "the good works Chloe planned in the state over which her husband ruled."[16] Once Beecher was in office, both he and Chloe Merrick Reed set out, as he put it, "to create a statewide system of education as efficiently and as rapidly as possible." In doing this, they wanted to make the schools a permanent part of everyday life, precluding any future conservative effort to undo their work. Earlier efforts under Chase and the Freedmen's Bureau focused largely upon African Americans. Any abridgment of the rights extended by Congressional Reconstruction threatened the future of a school system serving only African Americans.

It was apparent to both Charles and Chloe that if the school system obtained significant white involvement, then it would be much harder for any political group to dismantle it. To bring this about, Beecher and Reed based their appointments upon ability. "If no competent Republican could be found," the superintendent wrote, they made it their policy to "employ Conservatives [Democrats], if qualified, as County Superintendents." Beecher added, "a large part of the white population are Conservative, and it is important to secure their cooperation in educational movements."[17] One regionally oriented history of education in Florida acknowledged that Beecher and Reed's "county school officers were some of the best men in the state."[18] By recruiting talented local leadership, Charles and Chloe diffused objections to public education.

With hostility reduced, whites who wanted their children in schools began enrolling them. By the time of Beecher's last report to the governor on September 30, 1872, the rush to create schools had added almost another 200 to the system, which grew from 250 to 444. Corresponding with this increase, the number of students grew from 7,500 to 16,258.[19] Or, as Beecher put it, this number represented almost one-third of all Floridians between the ages of six and eighteen. The achievements of both Charles Beecher and Chloe Merrick Reed were even greater. Beecher stayed in office until January 23, 1873, and later that year his successor noted the existence of 511 schools and 19,196 pupils—this addition came as a continuation of their efforts.[20]

The successes of Charles and Chloe contributed to a paradox; the poorest and least populated southern state could count 50 percent of its school-age children enrolled by 1878. In the nineteenth century, Florida claimed to have the highest rate of literacy of any state of the old Confederacy.[21] Yet in 1866 Ansel Kinne had feared that traditional southerners would prevent the creation of an educational system in Florida. Congressional Reconstruction enfranchised blacks and brought his sister-in-law Chloe Merrick Reed and Charles Beecher to power. Together, they established a policy that reduced objections to schools. Swaim's notion of a "new heaven and new earth" became more than speculation.

Beecher's creative input for state government can be seen in his numerous reports to Governor Reed. He offered recommendations that later superintendents supported. As new schools opened, there was a great "want of textbooks." Or, as Beecher put it, "a large proportion of the people, if not the majority, are not able to buy [any]. Consequently, a large number of pupils are destitute of textbooks."[22] While the state had fulfilled part of its duty by approving a series of books, the books still needed to be purchased. Given the limited resources of the population, Beecher realized that this "must be done at public expense." He suggested that the books should be the "property of the county boards, for the use of schools, parents or guardians being held accountable for their loss or injury."[23] Problems with a lack of textbooks continued to annoy educators, and his successors found wisdom in his proposal. In 1881, for instance, a state superintendent found a classroom where twenty-seven children brought "twenty-three different kinds of textbook," many of which were "old and for the most part by different authors."[24]

The northern-born superintendent set his sights higher than mere primary and secondary education. When Beecher took office, the state had two small seminaries to address the needs of whites in higher education, and Florida also obtained approval from Congress for the charter of a new agricultural college. Yet the idea of having three separate schools did not seem wise to him: "It may be doubted whether, at the present stage of development and progress, Florida can sustain one institution worthy of being called a college or a university. To set up a common school and call it a college does not make it anything but a common school." This being the case, the legislation creating three separate schools seemed "a curse rather than a blessing. If any way can be devised to unite the three, so as to establish a university, with an agricultural collegiate department, then we might hope for success."[25] Although the state failed to follow this strategy, other experts in education reached the same conclusion. It should be noted, too, that while Beecher questioned the viability of a state agricultural college, he selected a governing board for it to maximize its chances of success. Among its leaders were the Democratic lieutenant governor, William D. Bloxham. Bloxham became an extraordinary figure in nineteenth-century Florida, winning the governorship twice.

Beyond these major recommendations, Charles also offered a series of suggestions to improve county school systems. He wanted the size of the school boards to be reduced from five members to three to increase "their efficiency and diminish expense," and he also called for a regular census of the number of school-age children in each county.[26] By having current knowledge of the number of children who were and were not attending, it would be easier to assess the progress that was being made. Although these proposals languished, a Democratic administration later reduced the number of school board members in many counties.[27]

Even though the Reed administration pursued many changes in education, it made no provisions for higher education for African Americans. Religious organizations were unwilling to let this situation persist, and the Baptists, the AME, and the Methodist Episcopal Church took up the challenge. Charles Pearce held a meeting to establish a black Methodist college in the summer of 1872, and John Swaim responded as well. In July of the same year, courses in theology were being offered for African Americans in Swaim's church. Reverend Samuel B. Darnell and his wife taught classes, enabling a supporter to boast that "we have our college and theological seminary already started."[28] In 1873 the school added a curriculum for students interested in education. By late spring, with Swaim's support, a meeting was held to formalize its organization.

On that occasion and with Swaim serving as chairman, a committee selected trustees and officers for Cookman Institute. While it has been described as "the first school of higher education of Negroes established in the State of Florida, and for a long time the only school of its kind in the state," this statement is somewhat misleading.[29] There were earlier attempts to organize schools, but none may have actually offered classes as quickly as Cookman. Such a rapid start can be attributed to both the local and national leaders among its trustees. This group included Calvin Robinson, Ossian B. Hart, a Methodist bishop, and the head of the denomination's freedmen's aid society.

Once initiated, the scheme for higher education for African Americans advanced rapidly. By 1876 it was reported that Cookman Institute had 60 pupils and needed space for an additional 100 to 140. A visitor to Cookman questioned a student in an algebra class and found knowledge "that would have done credit to pupils in any of our schools in the North."[30] By 1888 the school reported 167 students enrolled in its "academic and normal department," and "preparatory studies were offered in 'law, medicine, and the ministry'."[31] Cookman gave its students an "excellent" preparation, and they went on to leadership positions "in all sections of the South" and beyond.[32] Among its nineteenth-century graduates were four medical doctors in Jacksonville and L. W. Livingstone, U.S. consul to Haiti. In addition, the very well known AME bishop Abram Grant "read his primer" in the primary department, and the famous civil rights leader A. Philip Randolph graduated from an academic program in 1907.[33]

The excitement for educational advancement begun under Beecher's watch echoed initiatives sponsored by others. Florida lacked high schools, and citizens in Jacksonville clamored for one. In September 1874 a newspaper in the city reported the opening of Duval High School, with John Swaim's son, Matthias Freeman Swaim, as principal. His appointment was a popular one, and he was described in the newspaper as "a gentleman of fine education and culture [who] will fill the position with honor and dignity."[34] Matthias met the expectations raised by the press. Several years later the school was described in another newspaper as being held in "high esteem by the people, proof of the ability of the management."[35] Duval High School achieved an unusual reputation among the South's schools. In 1888 a survey of secondary schools found few that "compared favorably with schools in other states." The report noted, however, that "an exception to that should be made for the high school in Jacksonville. The quality of its programs was 'scarcely inferior to the colleges of the state'."[36]

Under John Swaim's leadership the Methodist Episcopal Church continued the pattern in education that it began with its churches. Just as the largely African American Zion M.E. Church predated the organization of the white Trinity Methodist Church, Cookman Institute predated the organization of Duval High School. To help insure the success of both schools, leaders recruited skilled educators from the ranks of northern clergy. Samuel Darnell was a graduate of Drew Seminary, now Drew University. Matthias Swaim had studied at Pennington Seminary, presently a New Jersey preparatory school.[37] By helping to establish important schools, Swaim continued to fulfill his commitment to a modern Florida based upon the meaningful participation of all its citizens.

Many of the extraordinary developments in education, at least those of Charles Beecher and Chloe Merrick Reed, depended upon Harrison Reed's remaining in office. His frustration with the Osborn political machine's 1868 impeachment attempt brought only a temporary respite, and the pressure returned. In the meantime, Milton Littlefield resurfaced in the lives of the Reeds. Littlefield had become an expert in financing railroads and in selling railway bonds. To the chagrin of residents of North Carolina, monies from his projects tended to disappear, and consequently the actual rail construction never matched the public promises. Nevertheless, Littlefield had skill and Reed put him to work. To forestall Osborn's renewed impeachment efforts, the governor proposed a truce and an exchange: Milton Littlefield and Reed would get a project passed by the legislature and Osborn would get his pet project, the Great Southern Railroad.

This swap offered the use of massive land grants from the state's internal improvement fund to finish the rail connections west from Tallahassee to Pensacola and Mobile (the Littlefield and Reed project) and to open up southern Florida through a company controlled by the senator's friends. To implement the first of these projects, Reed called a special session of the legislature in May 1870, during which four million dollars in bonds were transferred to Littlefield. One historian notes, "The passage of this act aroused intense opposition, and charges were made of corruption."[38] A citizen complained, "Taxes are getting to be enormous and all to enrich a lot of thieves who for the sake of office call themselves Republican."[39] Yet these fears went unrealized. A notice, published and circulated in New York, stated that the bonds "were issued without competent authority."[40] As a result, their sale collapsed.

This entire event still seems rather curious. Reed, as his critics claimed, could have been plotting with Littlefield to divert all of the funds and simply enrich himself. It is even more probable that Reed expected to reward Littlefield for his services and build the railroad. Why not become wealthy and be the Alexander Mitchell of Florida? Yet this interpretation, no matter how likely, still does not explain the notice that undermined the bond sale. Osborn's political machine might have been the source of the notice, but this seems very unlikely. By obstructing the deal, they would have ended the truce with Reed and jeopardized their own rail projects. It also seems improbable that Jacksonville's business community would have used its New York connections to scuttle the deal. Building the railroad would have brought new business to Jacksonville and enhanced their own opportunities. There is still another possibility. The unsavory nature of the special session may have deeply troubled Chloe Merrick Reed. Being a New Yorker herself, she had contacts who could have told her how to stop the bond sale. There is also the possibility that she forced Reed to terminate the matter. Under duress he may have issued the notice himself. Whatever the case, most bonds went unsold, and much of the corruption trumpeted by the press and by Democratic politicians never materialized.[41]

In any event, the matter damaged Reed. In particular, the various schemes to finance new railroads produced an unexpected consequence. It unsettled an investor, Francis Vose, who held Florida railway bonds. In an effort to protect their value and force David Yulee to pay his debts, Vose sought an injunction to limit the use of state land to back new railroad construction. While Reed had the option of fighting Vose's action, there were threats of renewed impeachment proceedings. The governor forestalled this effort by getting Yulee and his conservatives to help him. To do this, Reed promised not to oppose Vose—a decision that could block Osborn's Great Southern Railroad and enhance the profitability of Yulee's line. This possibility pleased the railroad executive and Yulee gained the governor time. Moreover, Reed thought that the courts would not seriously enforce the Vose injunction. Having let it come into being, Reed acted over the next year as if it did not exist.[42]

Senator Osborn took the Vose injunction more seriously than did the governor. In addition, the senator wanted a reappointment to another term. Having a friend as governor was essential to this process, and so the machine renewed its assault upon Reed. In the January session of 1872, Osborn's friends in the state legislature found "gigantic frauds" in Reed's and Littlefield's dealings. On February 10 the house impeached the governor. The charges, as a correspondent noted, were "high crimes and misdemeanors, in the overissue of bonds, embezzlement of public funds,

bribery, and corruption in office."[43] Pending a trial in the senate, the
house suspended Reed from office. This action meant that the lieutenant
governor, Samuel T. Day, would serve out the remaining months of
Reed's term.

Reed confounded his opponents by first staying at his home in South
Jacksonville and then reappearing in Tallahassee in early April. He went
to the governor's office while Day was not present and resumed his office.
Reed issued a "proclamation declaring Day's acts illegal and void" and
then sought the state supreme court's help.[44] A historian notes, "Reed's
grasp for power" shocked Osborn's machine. In a dither, they assumed
1868 was going to be repeated.[45] They feared that the court would rule
in Reed's favor, and they would lose yet again. To keep this from happen-
ing, Day called for a special session of the legislature to try the governor.
Then, to the machine's amazement, the court handed Day a victory. The
situation in 1872 was, in fact, different, and the charges against Reed had
been part of the regular session of the legislature. But the matter remained unresolved. Having called the legislature into session, Reed
pressed for a senate trial. Realizing that this could be dangerous, Osborn's team sought an adjournment to forestall further problems. In spite
of their efforts, pro-Reed Democrats blocked the machine, and on May
6 newspapers reported that the governor "was acquitted. Six Democrats
and four Republicans sided with the governor; three Democrats and four
Republicans opposed him."[46]

For a few weeks Reed seemed invincible. In a shocking fashion he had
vanquished his foes, and his decision to return to Tallahassee in April
occurred just before a Republican Party convention. News of Reed's
actions upset the meeting, and African Americans who had grown weary
of the political machine's heavy-handed use of bribery and whiskey to
gain allies rebelled. A black political leader demanded open voting and in
the confusion a number of Yankees abandoned Osborn. As a consequence, "the results were a major setback for the ring." "This event
showed," a newspaper reported, "the complete discomfiture of the infa-
mous coalition that has done so much to disrupt the party."[47]

Reed's celebration lasted only a few weeks. His failure to give the Vose injunction any credibility angered United States District Judge Philip Fraser. Rather than giving in to the governor's wishes, Fraser, a historian notes, appointed "a receiver for the fund, thus taking away the governor's control of revenues from state land sales. The judge also ordered the trustees' arrest, pending the court's hearing of contempt charges in December."[48] In a crushing blow, Reed lost the ability to use state property to finance railroad construction. This tied the governor's hands, and the Vose injunction blocked railroad development for a decade to come. To insure that Reed complied, Fraser required him to post a $5,000 bond. The Vose injunction cost the state its Internal Improvement Fund, one of its few assets in a weak economy.

Reed was shaken from this sudden turn of events, and his constant struggles with Osborn hurt his standing with African Americans. Charles H. Pearce, in particular, paid a heavy price. Rather than continuing to back the governor, the AME leader turned to a different leader. Ossian Hart was just as committed to African American education as Charles Beecher and Chloe Merrick Reed; plus the Unionist had stayed away from the financial schemes that hurt the governor's reputation. On July 4, 1872, Pearce organized an AME college in Live Oak and invited Hart to attend its founding ceremony. Giving a place of honor to the Unionist, the black Methodist asked him to speak "immediately after his own remarks."[49] The nonverbal communication signaled to hundreds of African Americans that Hart had begun to replace Reed in AME circles.

Special circumstances in Chloe Merrick Reed's life may have affected the train of events. The shift in Pearce's preferences came when Mrs. Reed, at the age of forty, was pregnant with her first child. With ties to members of the AME church herself, under normal conditions she might have had some influence on the decision. But, being less involved in state matters, she could not reassure Pearce of her husband's goodwill. The absence of her steady influence on Harrison Reed might also explain his next decision. During the state political conventions in the summer, the Republicans turned away from Yankees and nominated Hart, while the

Democrats selected Lieutenant Governor William D. Bloxham. To the governor, Bloxham was a man with promise. After almost two years in office, Charles Beecher agreed. Having come to know many of the state's leaders, he offered his sister Isabella an assessment that the young Democrat had "a better character than any I know on the Republican side."[50]

When the campaign began, Bloxham decided to court liberal Republicans, people who had grown weary of President Ulysses S. Grant and his wicked friends. To make his election even more certain, Bloxham distanced himself from the lost cause: "He argued that he wanted to bring all responsible factions together."[51] This meant that both former Confederates and those who had served under the star-spangled banner would work together to establish better government. Bloxham's strategy appealed to many Floridians, but he undercut it with a dull speaking style—something he improved in time. Hart, on the other hand, was older, and the rigors of traveling in frontier south Florida exhausted him.

As the election approached, Reed gambled boldly. He decided to use his power to elect Bloxham. Reed did this, according to a historian, by "placing the supervision of voting and the counting of returns in Democratic hands in many key counties."[52] In a close election the results could be tipped. For his actions, a political operative believed that Bloxham would secure Reed "a Senatorship."[53] Having remained near Andrew Johnson in thinking, the governor could then follow brother-in-law Alexander Mitchell and openly form an alliance with conservatives. He could gain a new lease on political power and simultaneously impress his millionaire relative. Reed's decision may have been kept from his wife, and he might have pursued the agreement with Bloxham without her approval. The odds are that she learned what he did, and then chose not to use her connections with African Americans to help him. Pearce, in turn, probably rejoiced in turning to Hart.

It took weeks to count the votes in the November 1872 election, and at first the outcome seemed to be in Bloxham's favor. But when the results were finally tallied, Hart had won. The margin of victory came from places of AME strength: "Most of the difference came from middle and north Florida's predominantly black counties." In Leon County, Pearce's forces added almost 900 votes; in Jefferson County, Robert Meacham "turned out an additional 861"; and in Jacksonville AME ministers "increased the tally by almost 600."[54]

The Hart victory proved as devastating for Reed as had the Vose injunction. When the Unionist came to Tallahassee for his inauguration in 1873, he was uncharacteristically mean-spirited and, reportedly, refused to let the outgoing governor and Chloe ride in the official carriage. The new governor then used his influence in the legislature to blunt Reed's election to the United States Senate and to end Osborn's bid for reelection. The senator received only six votes; Reed, only three. Reed's talent for daring gambles had betrayed him. Yankee political influence in the Republican Party waned, and African Americans exercised power directly or shared their influence with native-born southerners. While the Reed administration provided avenues for reformers, many had sought change outside of politics. With her pen Harriet Beecher Stowe pursued a transformation more lasting than the governor's schemes.

8

Palmetto-Leaves and Depression

While the Reed administration served as a vehicle for reform, Harriet Beecher Stowe sought to shape Florida's future with words. In the early 1870s brother Henry Ward Beecher provided a new forum for her and the family. Seeking to create a nondenominational journal that would appeal to a wide readership, he purchased a New York newspaper, the *Church Union*, expanded its content, and changed its name to the *Christian Union*. The Stowes enthusiastically endorsed these changes, and they agreed to supply the newspaper with columns every week. Calvin offered contributions from his studies of the New Testament, and she "from her love of travel, current events, and scriptural meditations."[1] With their writings interspersed between Henry Ward Beecher's sermons and editorials and many articles by their siblings, the *Christian Union* found success quickly. In a little over two years after its initial appearance in January 1870, circulation surpassed 80,000 copies.[2]

In the *Christian Union*, Stowe's concern for Florida became rapidly apparent, perhaps driven by a knowledge of the weaknesses of Reed's government. Starting in May 1870, and then again in February 1872, and continuing until August of the same year, she published eighteen different articles about Florida. She began by offering northern readers an analysis of people who should and should not come. She recommended Florida to four groups. First, she turned to those persons suffering from pulmonary diseases. If they "benefited from hot weather at the North," they might find becoming a permanent resident "the salvation of life."[3]

Beyond this group were those who suffered from rheumatic and neuro-logical conditions. "The climate," she wrote, "is soothing and sedative." While the weather in winter could be very changeable, the variations "were not so harsh and severe as in the northern States. There is more time [when] it is safe to be in open air." Stowe then recommended Florida to those who enjoyed nature and outdoor activities such as boating, fish-ing, and hunting. She described the scenery on small creeks as "a beau-tiful dream." The fourth group, as one might expect, included "industri-ous young men," those willing to plant citrus trees or other experimental crops. Within a decade they "might hope to realize a handsome indepen-dence."[4]

Having firsthand knowledge, Stowe also suggested that Florida would not appeal to everyone. The state is "raw" and "unsettled," she wrote. "Like all new countries it has many disadvantages, roughness, and hard-ships."[5] Therefore, she told the "discontented," those who lacked a pleas-ant disposition, to stay away. To this group she added still another. She was convinced that those whose lives were attached to city living would have difficulty in adjusting. It is likely that they "will perish with loneli-ness and pining for the active busy world they had left."[6]

Perhaps the most important article in the series also represented her most subtle approach. In May 1872, she chronicled agricultural experi-ments on her farm. The first year's effort was a disaster. On sandy soil with little or no fertilizer, the first crop of cucumbers did not pay the shipping charges to send it north. With the same poor preparation, heavy rains destroyed her cabbages. Yet the situation changed when she re-duced the size of the plots and added manure. By her fourth season four acres of cucumbers became only an acre and a half. Yet with proper fertilizer the plot grew, she reported, "four hundred bushels and brought a gross return of thirteen hundred dollars."[7] With two acres of cabbages, Stowe's farm received $500 gross, "of which three hundred would be clear profit." Two seasons of poor returns had been followed by two seasons of success. "We have," she wrote, "found our leading market crops, handsomely remunerative."[8]

The secret to her success, she insisted, was, in fact, no secret. The key proved to be manure and careful cultivation: "It is best to spend little for land and much for the cultivation of it." Or, expressed differently, to engage in vegetable production without fertilizer was to embark on a "leaky and surely sinking ship."[9] The significance of this discourse may be seen in the 1870 census. The entire state of Florida marketed only $32,000 worth of garden produce, and its orchard crops, including citrus, had a value of $52,000. A historian in 1902 concluded that as of 1870 "oranges had not risen to importance as a product for exportation."[10] Stowe's involvement in agricultural experimentation, rather than being a poor imitation of a widespread phenomenon, reflects her proximity to the origins of modern Florida. The numbers in the census report measure the innovations of John Swaim, Spencer Foote, and a handful of farmers near her home.

Stowe's articles provide a history of citrus production in Mandarin. She found that in five years' time frosts damaged the crops on two occasions. These were said to be the only losses since 1835, when a severe freeze killed the trees to the ground. According to Stowe, "Then they started up with the genuine pluck of a true-born orange tree, which never says die, and began to grow again. Nobody pruned them or cared much about them in any way, and you can see trees that have grown up in four, five, and six trunks."[11] Once the trees partially recovered, the "orange insect" nearly destroyed them all over again. With such frustrating developments, the farmers abandoned the trees to the forest. Since then, they became the "beautiful creatures they are." Many of them, she wrote, were thirty feet tall, "with spreading graceful tops and varnished green leaves, full of golden fruit."[12] In 1872 Stowe claimed that her 115 trees produced a crop of 60,000 oranges. A nearby neighbor's three immense trees each produced 5,000 oranges. In 1873 she reported that new groves were becoming common. There are "thousands of trees that have recently been set in this neighborhood."[13] The "golden flood" from the new trees would make the production of "our present groves of a few hundred trees" look like "nothing."[14]

Stowe added spice to her articles in the *Christian Union* by including basic tourist fare. On boating trips upon the river and nearby creeks, she observed flowers in profusion and gave careful attention to the blossoms of magnolias. Like other tourists she traveled to St. Augustine to see the Ancient City. This required a journey from "Tekoi" on a railroad of wooden rails. In 1872 horses pulled its best railroad car. If this were filled or not available, it left "the roughest things imaginable." The journey to the town took, to her surprise, only several hours. She extolled St. Augustine's many attractions. There were "narrow crooked streets" with "dark-browed people with great Spanish eyes."[15] Periodically she passed Catholic clergy and the occasional nun: "It is as if some little, old, dead, and alive Spanish town, with its fort and gateway and Moorish bell towers, had broken loose, and floated over here, and got stranded on a sand bank."[16]

The articles found their audience, and the public responded by writing Stowe letters. While many of these came from men seeking investment advice, they also came from women and children. Fifteen letters arrived in one week and in another came "a neat little pile of responses to our papers from all the States in the Union."[17] She even responded to the children's letters in a manner to interest them, relating the sad loss of her cats. Two had been mistaken by a neighbor's child as "rabbits" and had been shot. The valiant mother cat, Puss, protected a litter of kittens from a marauding dog only to have a leg broken. The concerns of women gave rise to other issues, but in a similar approach. In 1875, there were single women seeking employment opportunities who felt secure enough to write a famous author. Stowe responded by saying that a "competent dressmaker might find support here." In general, any woman "with well-defined talent and willing to work might be successful."[18] Opportunities in Florida existed for women as cooks in hotels and boardinghouses. Women could serve as companions for invalids. Stowe declared, "There is a great demand for skilled, intelligent labor in all the departments of household life."[19]

Stowe's efforts at promoting Florida came with warnings. The state, she told readers, had a wonderful winter season but three "formidable summer months, July, August, and September." In them the "heat is excessive and the liabilities of new settlers to sickness is great."[20] This combination meant that Florida would be most attractive to those persons who could have several homes. It "is peculiarly adapted to the needs of people who can afford two houses and want a refuge from the drain that winter makes on the health."[21]

Many of the articles in the *Christian Union* found subsequent circulation as a book. When *Palmetto-Leaves* appeared in 1873, it included an additional topic—labor relations in the South. The key to the future, according to Stowe, lay in schools: "The Negro children are bright; they can be taught anything."[22] It was, therefore, essential that education be made a priority—especially schooling that stressed useful skills: "The teaching in the common schools ought to be largely industrial, and do what it can to prepare the children to get a living by doing something well. Practical sewing, cutting and fitting, for girls, and the general principles of agriculture for boys, might be taught with advantage."[23] When the school in Mandarin burned in 1871, she urged its replacement: "To see people who are willing and anxious to be taught, growing up in ignorance, is the sorest sight that can afflict one."[24]

Some of Stowe's hopes for African Americans were quickly dashed by economic circumstances with state and national ramifications. In *Palmetto-Leaves* she urged them to live thriftily and save for the future. She rejoiced that the deposits of the Freedmen's Savings Bank had climbed to more than $31 million—a sum that reflected the hard work and industry of African Americans. This institution failed in 1874, however, undercutting her message and countless Americans who had sought to help blacks. In spite of the bank's obvious linkage to the federal government and the Freedmen's Bureau, Congress did not rescue it.

The 1870s became a time of economic depression; the boom that began in the Civil War ended when the noted financier Jay Cooke overspeculated in railroad bonds. Panic swept away banks and many lost fortunes. Stowe's biographer observes, "In the first year of the depression

alone, five thousand businesses failed."[25] When a recovery began a few
years later, yet another panic cut it down. In 1878, the famous author
wrote that a third of her investments were no longer productive. According to Stowe, her family lived by "sailing close to the wind and making
expenses as small as possible."[26] While she found comfort in the fact that
the principal had not been lost, economic trouble affected other family
members. Stowe's sister-in-law reported that Henry Ward Beecher was
"dreadfully depressed," feelings his niece's husband accentuated.[27] Beset
with financial woes, the husband had created a $30,000 certificate by
adding a zero to a $3,000 note. The discovery of this fraud led to bank-
ruptcy and a prison sentence.

Even in those perilous economic times, the tourists continued to ar-
rive in Florida. In May 1874, Stowe stated that 40,000 were in the Jacksonville area—a threefold increase since the beginning of the decade.
The remarkable boom in tourism explains why investors still built hotels.
A group came to the city in 1875 and spent $125,000 constructing and
furnishing the Carleton. Opening in an era of financial trouble, it became
"one of Florida's famous hotels."[28] Under better economic times in the
1880s, the state attracted from 48,000 tourists in the 1883–84 season to
65,193 in the 1885–86 season.[29]

The remarkable flood of visitors sustained the local economy in the
depression-riddled 1870s—an accomplishment that can be partly attributed to Stowe's efforts in publicizing the state. Interestingly enough,
having provided the economic spark that propelled modern Florida
through a national depression, Stowe continued writing about the state
in the *Christian Union*. This new series includes some eighteen articles
beginning in February 1873 and ending in April 1877. These additional
articles lend support to the suggestion that she intended to write a second
book about Florida. While the content occasionally covers old ground,
there are two extraordinary exceptions; the first is a vivid account of her
trip "up the Ocklawaha" and the second is her description of her journey
to Tallahassee in 1874. If Stowe had revised *Palmetto-Leaves* for a second
printing, she might have included these articles as new chapters.

The new material conveyed a sense of the romance, danger, and southern hospitality given the author of *Uncle Tom's Cabin*. Before her book *Palmetto-Leaves*, she had intentionally stayed away from the steamer that carried tourists from Jacksonville to Silver Springs. In March 1873 she cast aside her fears and went "on a bush-whacking tour through swamps of alligators."[30] In spite of her many reservations about that "suspicious looking craft," she boarded it. The little steamer proved to be a remarkable surprise: "We found a neat, well-ventilated cabin, with berths for eight ladies, as comfortable as could be desired."[31] The behavior of both the captain and the cook proved to be equally pleasant. While the table offered the twenty passengers only "the space of a handkerchief," the food was good. Stowe overcame her apprehensions, becoming an "uncritical devourer of whatever was set before her."[32]

The details of the trip fascinated readers. The steamer *Ocklawaha* left Mandarin before lunch and docked in Palatka around 7 P.M. During the next few hours the passengers retired to their bunks and fell asleep. "In the middle of the night we were wakened by the scraping of the branches against our little boat, and looked dreamily out to see that we were gliding through palmetto forests and weird grottoes, lit up with blazing pine torches. It seemed part of a fantastic dream as our weary eyes closed and the boat rippled on."[33] The next morning found the steamer in a forest. After breakfast the passengers sat on a platform in front of the wheelhouse to observe what could be seen: "Sometimes the whole way was given up to palmetto groves—rising in every conceivable shape and variety. The trunk of the palms sometimes seems a regular and exact pillar of basketwork, built up twenty or thirty feet. In the crevices large ferns and air plants take root, so that the tree is often a pillar of various foliage and flowers."[34] At other times the palms gave way to cypress trees of great height or still other species: "Growth seemed to have run riot here, to have broken into strange goblin forms." As one might have expected, the steamer came upon alligators and various birds: "The long necked water turkey sits perched gravely on the boughs overhead, or dives in the waters below." There were cranes of various kinds and several types of curlews.

Stowe was enthralled: "The dreamy wildness, the perfect strangeness of it all, its utter unlikeness to anything one has ever seen, inclines one to aimless reverie."[35]

Her narrative continued at a breathless pace. At times the steamer passed a landing in the forest or a few hunters. In homemade clothing and peaked hats, they were formidable in appearance: "They seemed a grave, taciturn, unsmiling race, long haired, bearded and roughly attired; with sallow complexion and dark eyes."[36] To the steamer they brought provisions for the cook and oranges for the passengers. As the day wore on, the weather became hot, giving Stowe and other women headaches. The men added to their discomfort by shooting at wildlife: "The cry, 'dar's a gator' was a signal for a perfect fusillade more dangerous to us than to the alligators, who generally dove and paddled off."[37] Many birds were not so fortunate. The men shot at them, distressing Stowe: "I did not want to see them fall, mangled and fluttering, under the awkward shots of some of our sportsmen."[38]

The second morning found the *Ocklawaha* in a savanna. As the day passed, the open grasslands gave way to a series of lakes. After stopping at several places, the captain told them that they would reach Silver Springs at 1 or 2 A.M. To see it, the passengers spent the evening sitting up: "We seemed floating through an immense cathedral whose white marble columns met in vast arches overhead and were reflected in the glassy depths below."[39] With torches as lights, many things could be seen: "Every trunk, and limb, and branch of the trees was of glistening whiteness, like ivory. The gray moss that streamed down seemed like veils of silver, and was of a wonderful profusion."[40] The light occasionally startled birds, who sailed off into the darkness, and one passenger even grabbed a water turkey who was too slow to flee.

At last they arrived at their destination: "About one o'clock we glided into Silver Springs run, and by two, we were all gathered on the lower deck, looking down into transparent depths that gave the impression that our boat was moving through air. Every pebble and aquatic plant we glided over seemed, in the torch light, invested with prismatic brightness."[41] After the steamer docked, the passengers retired to their bunks for the night. In the morning some of the tourists got into a small craft and drifted out over the springs: "We could see the fish darting hither and thither. The water had the crystalline clearness and the magical prismatic reflections which give such charm to the blue grotto at Capri."[42] After this spectacular sight the steamer began its journey home, likely a relief to the exhausted travelers.

The second new article of significance also related a journey, but a much different one. In April 1874 Stowe visited Tallahassee, ostensibly as a part of a tour held for Yankee investors. While she claimed to "have gone with the multitude," a factor in her visit was her brother Charles. After leaving public office, he lived quietly, hoping to show his farm to his sister. Before coming to Newport, she saw the nearby region: "It is a fine rolling country with high green hills and deep valleys, and beautiful clear lakes, suggesting in some faint degree that part of the Berkshire County in Massachusetts."[43] While the area seemed to be too cold for citrus or other tropical crops, it had potential for farming. Corn, cotton, and even wheat held promise. "This fine land," she thought, "is now in the market so cheap that the opportunity for investment should not be neglected."

Perhaps to her surprise, local residents showered her with hospitality. "In every case" their gardens "were thrown open to our inspection in the kindest manner, the owners coming out and offering to cut roses and lilies or other floral treasures for us." The quality of the blossoms impressed Stowe: "our hands were filled with buds and roses of the most perfect kind."[44] After a day of such pleasures, the community held a reception in the town hall. The building "was beautifully adorned with greens and flowers, so as to look like a perfect bower, and 'Welcome' in large gilded letters was the inscription that met the eye on entering."[45]

On the following day Stowe made a brief dash to Newport. Upon her return to Tallahassee, a photograph was taken upon the steps of the state capital. Southerners and Yankees posed, greeting the famous author. She concluded her article with words that eased the minds of interested but wary northerners: "Why should we not be friends? What earthly interest have we now to separate us? The interest of every new settler in Florida must henceforth be that of every old settler; we are helpers of one another."[46]

The April 1874 photograph shows a change in the state's political life. Rather than being greeted by Governor Ossian B. Hart, Stowe is approaching his replacement, northern-born Marcellus L. Stearns. Hart's campaign against Bloxham damaged his health, and he could not overcome pneumonia. His fifteen months as governor brought remarkable success, but after the exertions, he grew weaker. His lungs hemorrhaged on March 18, 1874. John Swaim spoke at the graveside during the funeral, saying farewell to an old and trusted friend.

In Hart's brief stay in office, the accusations of scandal ended, and the school system continued to expand. Charles Beecher's position as state superintendent of public instruction was assigned to former secretary of state Jonathan Gibbs, an African American educated at two of the North's finest colleges. Under his able leadership the school system grew until there were 557 schools, reaching a third of all school-aged children in the state. In spite of illness, Hart delivered on his promises to Charles Pearce and added to the lives of African Americans by passing legislation to protect their civil rights. It was a tragedy for Florida that it lost the able, honest, and thoughtful leadership of its Unionist governor. With the reduction in political strife, there were Confederate sympathizers who concurred with Stowe about the possibility of friendship between southerners and Yankees. Even the embittered editor of the *Tallahassee Floridian* published articles claiming that "a new era appears to be dawning."[47]

Writers in New Jersey reinforced Stowe's success at attracting tourists. While John Swaim ended his publishing efforts in the early 1870s, others continued penning articles for the *Newark Sentinel of Freedom*. During the difficult economic years there were no shortages of Florida materials. Two stories appeared in 1873, five in 1874, thirteen in 1875, and three in 1876.[48] The largest series came from an anonymous correspondent who explored much of the state, both the destinations of tourists and the places to which they seldom strayed. This writer posted articles from Mandarin, Orange Lake, Ocala, Silver Springs, several places along the St. Johns River, and towns both east and west of Tallahassee. He found people near Mandarin who followed Stowe's example: "[They] have set out acres of orange trees, all of which will soon be bearing, have erected a good house with their own hands, have opened a store and are now in a fair way to make a fortune. Their industry is astonishing, their management admirable. They had but small means and have fairly carved an independence out of the wilderness."[49] The *Sentinel* correspondent visited the Stowes' home and found Mandarin to be delightful. As he put it, it was a "little gem." He did not question why she had come but rather why other poets had not joined her. He concluded that Mandarin was worthy of "all that can be said."[50]

The articles in the newspapers also created some unintended consequences. Being in Florida could help people in the early stages of consumption, but it did little for the desperately diseased—a fact that Stowe carefully told readers. Yet her warnings did not keep such people from coming. In the winter of 1872, two invalids came to Jacksonville. Finding the boardinghouses and hotels full of guests, they died alone, one in a street and the other in a privy. Such shocking events led to the formation of St. Luke's Hospital, one of Florida's first real hospitals. A charity to provide care to the destitute ill, the organization grew out of the activities of three local women. Soon, however, it caught the attention of Martha Reed Mitchell.

To help the hospital, Mitchell gave benefits at her estate. On March 30, 1876, for instance, 500 guests came to Villa Alexandria. It took three steamboats to carry them across the St. Johns River. Once at the house, attendees found "fancy articles" from Mitchell's travels. While many of these items were sold privately, a friend auctioned the rest in the evening. For those who enjoyed sweets and other refreshments, there were four tables in the dining room. Ice cream could be found on a porch along "with all the delicacies imaginable."[51] To encourage sales, newspapers reported that "all the prices were very moderate." In the evening guests strolled the estate's grounds with the help of "Chinese Lanterns" and flaming torches. To entertain them in the afternoon, the St. James Hotel supplied its orchestra, and in the evening Martha Reed Mitchell added singers and a band.[52]

Generosity such as Mitchell's did not escape Stowe's notice. The famous author enjoyed the estate's garden and its ninety-five different types of roses. Both women shared a love of flowers and a high regard for the Episcopal church, another cause that received their support. In 1877 Stowe repaid Mitchell's efforts by writing an article about Villa Alexandria. The famous author did so while hoping to rechannel investment in Florida. Immigration appeals were succeeding, but too many people came south and spent the minimum on winter housing. Or, as Stowe put it, they planned "to buy the very cheapest place and put the least possible amount of money into it."[53]

To widen the horizons of Yankees, Stowe described for them the Mitchell estate in intimate detail. When the millionaire came to South Jacksonville, she purchased "an old dilapidated plantation with less than a hundred orange trees." The edge of the river was low and marshy, and the buildings were "worthless." Mitchell covered the marsh with boatloads of oyster shell and white sand. Then she replaced the old house with "a charming villa, built in the Italian Swiss style, with broad verandahs and a picturesque tower."[54] Surrounding the house she planted the finest of domestic and imported trees and plants. According to Stowe, these were "date and cocoa palms from Egypt and West Indies, teas from Assam, and pines from California and Italy, California nutmegs, eucalyptus, tulip and Judas trees, Cape and Arabian jasmine, tree fern; spireas, azaleas, wisteria, hydrangeas, every variety of shrub, tree, and climbing rose, all flourishing in gorgeous splendor."[55] Beyond the gardens, a hundred orange trees had become thousands. The new ones came into production as the old responded to the finest care. To sustain this paradise, Mitchell had installed an irrigation system: "A windmill is constantly employed in raising water into large tanks, whence hose pipes can distribute it where it is needed."[56] Stowe went on to say that beach cottages in the North produced little income. Yet a generous investment in a winter home in Florida could be repaid with interest.

Harriet Beecher Stowe's article about Villa Alexandria placed the author in the midst of neighbors with northern roots. While her brother participated in the Reed administration, Stowe enjoyed the hospitality of the governor's sister. The Beechers and the Reeds were linked together in multiple dimensions, bound together in their desire to transform Florida.

9

The Twentieth Century Envisioned

While the remainder of the 1870s was a time that veered from great hope to great despair for the Reeds, the former governor made an effort to shape Florida intellectually. Leaving office in January 1873, the Reeds settled on their farm in South Jacksonville. Within months the depression began, and like millions of Americans they were ill prepared. Rather than enriching himself in public office, Reed left Tallahassee with debts. He claimed that these were the product of legal fees, a result of defending himself against impeachment attempts. A Democratic newspaper in Syracuse offered a different rumor. It suggested that Milton Littlefield had cheated the Reeds. Whatever the case, their finances remained precarious, and they lost their home in Tallahassee through foreclosure on April 3, 1876.[1]

Despite such a dismal backdrop, Chloe Merrick Reed attempted to create a pleasant home for herself, the former governor, and their child. There is evidence of her success in the recollections of a neighbor: "The Reeds had a small son, Harrison M. Reed, and he and I had good times romping around the big house and exploring the estate."[2] A tolerant and loving mother, Chloe indulged the children's interest in cats: "They were all kinds, mostly scrubs or the common alley variety, but we loved them dearly, dressed them up, put paper boots on them, and fed them until they were as fat as butter."[3] Their fun with their pets was eventually disrupted when David Mitchell came to live with his grandmother at Villa Alexandria: "He had a couple of ferocious bulldogs which he trained to catch and kill cats. This, to Harrison and me, was the height of cruelty, and we were not very fond of the little heathen." Watching her son grow to manhood brought Chloe much joy. Yet in the 1870s she bore two children who died—not uncommon in an age of high infant mortality.[4] By delaying marriage to the age of thirty-seven, she reduced the number of pregnancies and the number of children to mourn.

While family preoccupied Chloe Merrick Reed, Harrison's ambitions burned brightly. Still seeking an avenue to shape Florida and his future, he focused his attention on publishing. In September 1875 he began editing a new monthly magazine, *The Semi-Tropical*, with a very ambitious agenda. Beyond supplying advice for farmers, immigrants, and investors in Florida, he sought to create a "medium of discourse" for scholars, vacationers, and the physically infirm. To address the needs of a broad but educated audience required the writing of a sizable periodical. In 1876, for instance, each issue averaged sixty-four pages, with few advertisements. Besides such columns as "Fruit Culture," "Stock Raising," household advice, and "Timely Topics," it offered poetry, a serial novel, and descriptions of places in Florida seldom visited by tourists. To secure enough articles, Reed turned to some of the state's leading writers. These included Solon Robinson, a former newspaper reporter whose works appeared in the *New York Tribune*, and Ellen Call Long, the daughter of an early governor and protégé of Andrew Jackson.

To please such contributors and to meet the expectations of sophisticated readers presented Reed an additional requirement. The *Semi-Tropical* had to display technical quality in typesetting, paper, and layout. With years of experience as a newspaper editor and publisher, Reed had many talents to use. To further heighten the challenge and the likelihood of the magazine's success, he sent complimentary copies to newspapers in Chicago, New York City, Boston, Kansas City, and Philadelphia. Not to slight smaller cities, the journal also found its way to Knoxville, Tennessee; Madison, Wisconsin; Reading, Pennsylvania; Toledo, Ohio; Rutland, Vermont; Springfield, Massachusetts; and Baltimore, Maryland. Given Reed's connections to the Beechers and to John Swaim, reactions from the *Christian Union* and the *Sentinel of Freedom* came swiftly. The *Christian Union* mentioned the content of the *Semi-Tropical* and added the belief that "if the editor has the courage to stick to his subject and to protect his pages [from] real estate agents, he can make an excellent subscription list in the North." The Newark paper, for its part, praised the magazine's appearance: "It is the best specimen of typography we have seen from the South."[5]

Positive reactions also came from other newspapers, auguring a successful future for the magazine. The *Chicago Tribune* responded by saying that it "presents a varied and excellent table of contents." The *Boston Daily News* agreed and suggested that if people were debating moving west or south, they should get "the *Semi-Tropical* and study Florida."[6] The *Brooklyn Daily Eagle* proclaimed, "Florida is destined to become one of the most prosperous states in the South, and in a few years it will be able to furnish the entire country with abundant supplies of lemons, oranges, pineapples, and bananas. The *Semi-Tropical* has good work before it."[7] Reactions to the magazine's technical sophistication came in as well. The *New York Home Journal* noted, "the paper is good, the typography is fine, and the articles have a sterling ring to them."[8]

Following this dramatic start for his journal, Reed pursued its publication with a concern for high quality. Recognizing its merit, authors turned to the magazine as a forum for their ideas. In February 1876, Solon Robinson suggested that the Swiss offered a model for Florida to emulate. Their "magnificent roads, fine hotels, the care and attention bestowed upon travelers are all for a purpose; for the Swiss live on the money of travelers, and are wise enough to know that the easier and pleasanter they make traveling for tourists, the more of them will come, and the more money will be spent."[9]

Using this principle, Robinson believed that the city of Jacksonville should change. It was insufficient to improve just St. James Park in the town's center. Rather than stopping with such a modest project, the city should pursue a grander vision. The low marshy areas should be removed, replaced with "paving and ornamental streets, and making attractive parks or places of pleasant resort for invalids and other visitors." Money spent on such projects would be returned. It would be "repaid in the increase of pleasure seekers and money spenders, and the advance of property [values].[10]

Then, following Robinson's lead, writer A. S. Baldwin traced the history of another important issue, one affecting Jacksonville's growth as a transportation center. Problems arose with the entrance of the St. Johns River and a sandbar whose location and size changed constantly. At times it narrowed and at other times it grew to 400 feet or more in width. Sometimes the sandbar moved north and then south, migrating as much as three miles. Efforts to understand this phenomenon perplexed even the pilots who guided ships into the river. The situation was further complicated by tides and currents that swept along the coast and by the presence of a small river nearby. In any case, the problem meant that ships with seventeen feet of draft could enter the river on some occasions, while on others a ship drawing only ten feet would have trouble. Baldwin went on to recommend a system of jetties to block the coastal currents that carried sand into the river channel. He believed that solving problems with the river were "paramount to all local interests."[11]

The publication of such provocative articles led to an interesting development: by 1877, both Harriet Beecher Stowe and Charles Beecher chose the *Semi-Tropical* as a place for their ideas. The celebration of the nation's centennial created speculation about the country's future, and Charles began writing about an imagined Florida at the bicentennial. Beecher began his fictional trip to the 1970s in Jacksonville by choosing to travel by rail rather than by air. His Florida of the future was encircled by a rail line, the "Rim Road," which bound the state together with "flashing steel." Journeys could also be made by the new airline, "just opened in opposition to the old Air Ship line whose rates have been latterly considered rather exorbitant."[12] The presence of air travel changed the lives of Americans. Important men and women lived wherever they wished, and "many of the magnates of the general government had semi-tropical winter residences."[13]

In Beecher's fictional account, Florida became densely populated. As he journeyed down the Atlantic coast, he spent a "day or two at several of the chief cities on our route, especially New Smyrna and Miami."[14] Along the way, he thought of visiting "Canadian friends now residing at Everglades," a "paradise" where a vast watery region had been.[15] Then he lingered along Biscayne waters and traveled to Key West, where he conversed with a woman completing a voyage around the world. Her ship had gone from New York to Liverpool, through the Suez Canal to Canton, China. Then it crossed the Pacific, passing through the Panama Canal at Darien. Later, at a reception, Beecher talked with a U.S. senator from Mexico. Their discussions ranged from the successful banning of warfare to the curing of malaria. "Fevers once the bane of hot countries" were now "unknown."

The next morning, in his fictional account, Beecher resumed his travels on "the sumptuous Rim Road palace car" and stopped "over a day each at Charlotte Harbor, Manatee, Tampa, and Cedar Key." His journey ended at the Pavilion of the Gulf, a resort located off the coast: "Conceive of an immense edifice erected on piles driven, or screwed rather, deep into the bottom, so that the waves can freely dash between and under the floor of the lower story! This is owing to the tidal waves that sometimes set in from the Gulf in a southerly gale, rising to a height of ten feet or more. No structure, however firm, could stand the shock; but between these piles they rush harmlessly. All the wharves, docks, railways, warehouses, public and private buildings, are constructed in the same manner. It is like another Venice, a city of the sea. Long, wide streets without a foot of terra firma; traversed by innumerable small craft, among which is the recently introduced gondola. No wonder a place so unique in its character should be thronged with visitors from every part of the world."[16] While at the resort, Beecher talked with older men who remembered hearing how the whole state had been a wilderness: "no air lines; no railroads; and no Ocean and Gulf Canal."[17]

As a result of the state's growth, Beecher thought that the Everglades would no longer exist. Southern Florida would be the home of a large population of Yankees and Canadians. With a flair for such speculation, Charles sent drafts of his papers to Mandarin before sending them on to

Reed. While Stowe may have been amused at some of his ideas, she quickly recognized the effects of Florida's development upon wildlife. As early as 1873, she became frustrated with tourists who journeyed south and instantly became would-be hunters. An example of the carnage can be found in her nephew's account of his visit to the state.

When Henry Ward Beecher's son, William Constantine, came to Newport in the middle of January 1871, he started hunting. The slaughter began with a pileated woodpecker and the wounding of three red-winged blackbirds and ended on March 23, with the killing of a yearling buck. His trophies included two cardinals (January 20), "two new varieties of woodpeckers" (January 24), one sparrow hawk (January 24), one "large white heron" (February 27), one mud hen (February 27), one female water turkey (February 27), one bluebird (March 3), three nuthatches (March 6), several partridges, and perhaps a dozen ducks. William shot at and missed alligators, hawks, two pelicans (March 2), and a fish eagle. Some of these efforts may reflect Beecher's interest in taxidermy, and he mentions preserving some of his "kill." Yet shooting an otter "in the face" (January 18) and a tomcat (February 11) suggests something other than sportsmanship.[18]

Keenly aware of such behavior, Harriet Beecher Stowe saw grave problems arising in the future. The vast scale of development, suggested by Charles Beecher, would change modern Florida into a demon, destroying the state she loved. Alarmed at the prospect, she sought to communicate with other influential Floridians and the state legislature. Writing in the *Semi-Tropical*, she described the disgraceful behavior of tourists: "The decks of boats are crowded with men, whose only feeling . . . seems to be a wild desire to shoot something." If these were real hunters, there could be an allowance for their behavior: "But to shoot for the mere love of killing is perfect barbarism, unworthy of any civilized man."[19] The answer for Stowe lay in legal action: "Unless some protection shall be extended over the animal creation, there is danger that there may be a war of extermination waged on our forests."[20]

To drive home her message, she noted the rapid decline in all types of birds in the Mandarin area. As the situation deteriorated, she wondered if many might disappear. To win the sentiments of readers, she reminded them of the beauty of birds and carefully outlined their usefulness: "Guided by unerring instinct they pick the corn worm from its green shell—they find the burrows and holes where the eggs of destructive insects are hid and pick them out."[21] Wasn't the mockingbird a line of defense against hordes of grasshoppers? They are "God's own police, meant to search out and keep down the noxious . . . animal life."[22] What might happen to the new orange groves if the orange insect returned? "Is it not safer to protect the birds?"

With the publication of Stowe's article in January 1877, the *Semi-Tropical* emerged as a force in public affairs. Corresponding with this view, Reed reported that the bill to protect birds had "passed in the Senate" but only left the assembly in a weakened form.[23] Not discouraged with this result, he thanked Stowe for her efforts and promised to continue to press for stronger legislation. The subsequent submission of her article about Villa Alexandria in August confirmed his hope that the *Semi-Tropical* was the place for dialogue about the state's future.

In the spring of 1878, Reed abruptly stopped printing his magazine. Although an intellectual success, it may not have been a commercial one. The nation's economy remained troubled, and the number of sophisticated residents of Florida probably could not support such a venture. The end of the *Semi-Tropical* might have grown out of Reed's finances, or it might have been caused by the problems of its publisher, Charles W. Blew. Blew's mismanagement of the federal customs house, his other occupation, became a public scandal. It has been claimed by traditional southerners that they were victimized by unscrupulous northerners in the Reconstruction. But if Littlefield cheated the Reeds and then Blew hurt them, there is unfortunately a broader message. The unscrupulous victimized both Southerners and talented Yankees—a price paid by all.

The collapse of the *Semi-Tropical* gave Reed little choice but to rely upon his farm and the agricultural innovations he practiced. He was a force in the state from his appointment as postal agent until his magazine died, a period covering thirteen years. In 1878 his influence slipped away, although his ambition remained—dreams of wealth and power in a revi-

talized Florida outlasted both his tenure in public office and his magazine.

Congressional Reconstruction ended with a compromise that grew
out of the elections of 1876. To retain the presidency, Republicans forged
a deal with Democrats. The former received the electoral votes from
southern states such as Florida, while the latter got the governorship.
This decision resolved the close race between Republican Marcellus
Stearns and Democrat George Drew. Reed's support of Bloxham hurt his
chances of obtaining another important state position within his party,
and Democrats limited them as well. Drew, to make matters worse, pursued moderate policies and pleased Harriet Beecher Stowe with his state-
ments on behalf of education. Opportunities for Republicans continued
to exist, but many of these were at the local level. The end of Congressional Reconstruction did not keep Yankees or African Americans from
holding public offices in Florida. Citizens elected more persons of color
after 1876 than before.[24] In the rest of the 1870s and 1880s, Reed dabbled
in politics, but the potential had been reduced and he met little success.

While the ex-governor struggled, Stowe's interests changed, with a
lessening of her aggressive pursuit of a Florida filled with northern immigrants. She enjoyed being a grandmother and, as she aged, family
became even more important to her. She also found avenues to meet the
family's financial needs outside of writing. The lecture circuit, for instance, produced a "thousand dollar check" in 1873. With such opportunities, her efforts in writing slowed. In 1877 her columns about Florida
in the *Christian Union* came to an end. The last, in April, described the
circumstances of Native American prisoners in the fort at St. Augustine.
It was preceded by one in January that noted that "three new hotels have
been built in Jacksonville, and all are beginning to fill up." With Reconstruction at an end, she found that the transition had gone smoothly:
"Florida is all serene in politics as in nature."[25]

From the Stowes' porch at Mandarin, the need to strengthen modern
Florida no longer seemed crucial. By the early 1880s, the few families at
Mandarin had become 1,200 people. There were three stores, an equal

number of churches, many houses, and wharves. As the community grew, experimentation with early vegetables continued. It was reported that even Bermuda onions joined "bushels of Irish potatoes as well as numerous crates of tomatoes, cucumbers, and beans."[26] Corresponding with the growth, there were times when twenty bags of mail were dropped off at the town.

As Harriet Beecher Stowe came to the end of the 1870s, she published an article about Florida in the *Atlantic Monthly*. She had described her life in Mandarin in *Palmetto-Leaves* and in the *Christian Union*, yet she had not shared her first experiences. To fill this gap, she turned to the cotton plantation and Fred's misadventures. After having had a dozen years to adjust to the disaster, she felt comfortable in sharing it. Stowe followed the *Atlantic Monthly* article by writing another retrospective piece in the *National Review*. Published in two parts, it traced the origins of African American education. Stowe began by noting the experiences of Prudence Crandell in Canterbury, Connecticut. When Crandell opened a school for African American girls in 1832, she found intense hostility. A mob insulted her children and vandalized the building. Careful to cite problems in the North, Stowe added that the state "legislature passed an act making this school an illegal enterprise, and under this act Miss Crandell was imprisoned in the county jail." The attitudes behind these actions were dismal; African Americans were said to be "incapable of culture, education, and self-guidance."[27]

Having cited a negative example, she turned to many successes. She described the efforts of educators at Berea College in Kentucky, Howard University in Washington, D.C., Fiske University in Nashville, and Hampton Institute in Virginia. The achievements at these places were being accompanied by a change in heart among Southerners. The governor of Florida described efforts to prepare African Americans for "all the sacred duties" of citizenship as a "responsibility from which we can not escape."[28] Yet the potential was hurt by the lack of resources and the consequences of the Civil War. Stowe, then, boldly urged the use of federal support: "Our national government should grant to the impoverished Southern States the funds to carry through a universal system of education."[29] Investments in education would yield a vast return and encourage respect for the law and "for the mutual rights of the races."[30]

As Stowe addressed major issues and wrote less about the state, her sister-in-law published a book about Florida in 1879. Eunice Bullard Beecher, Henry Ward Beecher's wife, had visited Charles in 1871 and purchased land on Kingsley's Lake for her daughter's children in 1877. With this background and other trips, she wrote *Letters from Florida*. Using Charles as an example, Eunice Beecher noted the miraculous changes in his health. When he came to Newport, her brother-in-law had been "a feeble gray-haired man, over whom the doctors had pronounced the sentence of death."[31] Able at first only to sit in a chair and give instructions, he began to regain strength. Rather than remaining idle, he began to work—"at first only a few moments at a time."[32]

As the months passed, his endurance increased, and he labored even longer. When Eunice Beecher came to Florida in 1871, she found him transformed. On the eve of his appointment to state office, he was "vigorous and full of energy and resolute industry."[33] His service in government must have been very agreeable, too. When Eunice saw Charles in 1874, she felt that no man could be found more energetic and happy. Not content with improving his orange trees, he turned his attention to other crops. Making his farm at Newport a miniature Mandarin, he raised Irish potatoes and "all kinds of vegetables."

While traveling to Newport, Eunice Beecher visited a place that rivaled Silver Springs for beauty. When one looked down into the fabled Wakulla Springs, fish that appeared close to the surface were actually twenty feet deep: "The water is of the most marvelous transparency. I dropped an ordinary pin in the water, forty feet deep, and saw its head with perfect distinctness as it lay on the bottom."[34] The success of the experiment led to another, and a dime could be seen after it sank almost two hundred feet, something "incredible."

When Eunice Beecher published her *Letters from Florida* in 1879, Yankees were leaving the banks of the St. Johns to spread out into the interior. She observed, "Pretty settlements are springing up around beautiful lakes."[35] From unpromising beginnings, orange groves were "coming into bearing." Success at pioneering work yielded comfortable homes and well-dressed families. For those in the North who were in poor health or of very limited means, Florida offered the potential of abundant life.

After the publication of Eunice's book, the Beechers joined the Reeds and Swaims in becoming less active as leaders of modern Florida. When Eunice Beecher's book appeared, she was sixty-seven, the same age as Harrison Reed, and Harriet Beecher Stowe was slightly older. What is surprising is not that leadership soon passed to a younger generation, but that it had been held for so long by people born between 1806 and 1815. The time for new leaders, however, came.

In January 1880, public attention turned to Jacksonville with the visit of former President Ulysses S. Grant. The town offered Grant a celebration worthy of any northern city. Thousands lined the streets, cheering, waving handkerchiefs, and throwing bouquets. A newspaper claimed that "everywhere along" a parade route such "enthusiasm was manifest."[36] In the spirit of the occasion, Democrat Governor George Drew and his cabinet became full participants. In the banquet that followed, warm compliments came to both the former president and the state's chief executive. A speaker hoped that Grant would be "blessed with the fullness of days and a bountiful store of God's richest blessings."[37] Another speaker told the audience that Drew had given Florida high-quality leadership: "He has governed with integrity, ability, and fidelity."[38] When the festivities ended, one newspaper concluded: "Yesterday was certainly the greatest day that this city has ever witnessed."[39]

Grant and his party, including reporters from New York and Chicago, left Jacksonville on January 8 by steamboat for Sanford. As the vessel passed Mandarin, countless eyes turned to get a glimpse of the Stowe house and the town. On January 10, this same group saw the former president begin the Florida Southern Railroad by digging the first shovel of earth. While this line would connect Henry S. Sanford's development projects—hotel and orange groves—to Orlando some twenty miles away, it also linked the developer to other figures in Florida's future. The Florida Southern Railroad would, in time, become a property of railroad magnate Henry B. Plant. Among Plant's early partners was, of course, Henry M. Flagler.[40]

In the early 1880s, Flagler changed his thinking about the state—a crucial event for Florida's future. In 1878, he had brought his ailing wife, Mary, to Jacksonville. Once in the town, he found little to do other than walking between the hotels. Biographer David Chandler suggests that the Flagler family saw "soft blue sky mingling with the fragrant orange groves."[41] Unhappy with the town, the Flaglers sailed to Tocoi and traveled on to St. Augustine. Their experiences in the ancient town proved unpleasant: "The accommodations were very bad, and most of the visitors were consumptives."[42] Ignoring the doctor's advice, Henry Flagler convinced his wife and family to leave. Or, as Chandler puts it, "the life of Standard Oil was more important" than that of Mary Flagler. Her future required living in Florida, and "he refused."[43] Yet, in spite of these experiences, when Henry Flagler himself became ill in 1882, he returned to the state—a trip that preceded a honeymoon journey with his second wife in November 1883.

This time, rather than being upset with accommodations in St. Augustine, he found the new San Marco "one of the most comfortable and best kept hotels in the world."[44] Instead of staying in the gardens, he joined other men of his social class: "I couldn't set still all of the time. I used to take walks down St. George Street, around the plaza to the club house, and then back to the hotel. I found that all the other gentlemen did the same thing, with apparent regularity and then, as now, that was all there was to do for recreation and amusement."[45]

Henry Flagler found these experiences agreeable. As a partner of John D. Rockefeller, he annually received a princely fortune. Even though he remained a director of Standard Oil into the twentieth century, Flagler began turning his responsibilities over to younger men. As he freed himself from running a vast corporation, he began a second career. By 1885, he had resolved to turn St. Augustine into, as he put it, the "Newport

[Rhode Island] of the South."⁴⁶ To make it the most fashionable resort of
the era required building one of the country's great luxury hotels, the
Ponce de Leon.

As workers constructed the hotel, Flagler sought to modernize rail
connections. Joining a company building a new line from Jacksonville to
St. Augustine, he spent $200,000 on an engine and tender. By the end of
1885, Flagler bought out the other owners. Wanting to cater to the very
wealthy, he wouldn't tolerate the inefficient Florida operations of the
past. Yet the transformation of these rail connections added to Flagler's
new interests. No longer confined by the narrowness of Standard Oil, he
changed as a person. The creation of grand hotels with the artistry to
appeal to the most refined tastes awakened Flagler's own talent. Growing
in breadth and depth, he shifted away from money as the "center of his
view."⁴⁷

As Flagler extended his rail lines and hotels south, several events
changed modern Florida. The benign weather patterns that had per-
sisted since 1835 broke. In 1880, for instance, temperatures in the twen-
ties damaged the trees, and a freezing rain destroyed the oranges. One
historian says that Harriet Beecher Stowe "wept at the destruction" in
Mandarin.⁴⁸ "Her entire orange crop was gone; she felt not only the loss
of the beauty and the pleasure of the grove, but also the revenue on which
she had come to rely."⁴⁹ The havoc of December 1880 was slight compared to the winter of 1894–1895. A different historian observes, "The
great freeze wiped out of existence a hundred million dollars worth of
property in a night, and men walked the streets with stricken faces and
discouraged hearts."⁵⁰ The destruction killed the trees and even the stock
in nurseries, complicating efforts to replace dead groves.

In the midst of this disaster, a person sent Flagler undamaged lemon
blossoms from Miami. Recognizing that the freeze had not reached that
far south, he "carried his railroad to Miami" and then "built the town."⁵¹
For farmers still wanting to invest in citrus and winter crops, the message
was equally clear. Moving much further south, leaving Jacksonville and
Mandarin, reduced the threat of frosts and freezing weather.

The flight from Jacksonville was accelerated by an immense fire on

May 3, 1901. In a period of heat and drought, winds transformed a blaze into a firestorm. David Mitchell's account is extraordinary: "I had been over in town in the morning, and as I left to catch the boat across the river for the trip to Villa Alexandria, I passed the fire station. The alarm sounded and Chief Haney steamed out in the big red go-devil of a fire truck, drawn by two handsome bay horses of the fire department. It was just 12 o'clock. It was a hot day, and I remember thinking to myself, 'Well, Chief Haney has picked out a hot day, with heat rising in layers from the streets, for a fire, and I hope it does not last long'."[52]

Mitchell went home, "four miles from the Jacksonville Ferry, and as lunch was served, said to the butler, 'Pearson, what makes it so dark? Is there an eclipse of the sun?' He went to the north window and looked towards Jacksonville, and rushed back with a tense face, 'By God, Master David, it sure looks like the end of the world. Come, look!' There was a clump of imported bamboo at least forty feet high growing on the lawn about twelve feet from the north window, above that a pall of smoke obscured the sun and made it dark as night."[53]

By 2 o'clock Mitchell returned to the ferry slip and took the last boat across to the Jacksonville side. David Mitchell found the city wharf, "filled with precious belongings of Jacksonville's citizens, who hoped in vain to gain transportation to the south side of the river. There were family portraits, clothing, bric-a-brac, baskets of silver, trunks filled with heirlooms and precious documents and papers, and the people with their panic stricken faces as the fire leaped by bounds to the water's edge!"[54]

Leaving the wharf, Mitchell walked to a friend's home. From there he could see "two big hotels, the Windsor and the St. James, flames from the roofs, a million dollars going up in flames, but what a magnificent sight, the two big buildings made as they yielded their greatness to the fire!"[55] The conflagration also consumed the Carleton Hotel, John Swaim's home and churches, Cookman Institute, the city hall, the county court-house, 148 city blocks, and more than 2,000 buildings. The smoke could be seen in Savannah. When it was over, the resort city, John Swaim's town, no longer existed.

While the freezes and the great fire separated modern Florida from its place of birth, public sentiments obscured its founders. Northerners in the Reconstruction became "carpetbaggers"; all Yankees were transformed into Littlefields. Few remembered the contributions of the Swaims and the Reeds. Even the efforts of the Beechers and the Stowes became obscured, and as this happened the contributions of Henry Flagler loomed even grander. Modern Florida came to be seen as his creation. He became, in the eyes of the general public, its founder.

10

The Cast Exits

Suffering and Glory

When Henry Flagler returned to Florida in 1882, all but one of our reformers still lived, and they continued to do so for more than a decade. As the Reeds, Charles Beecher, and Harriet Beecher Stowe became elderly, they did become, to varying degrees, more physically feeble. But they were extraordinary people, and their extraordinary lives continued to unfold. One lived to the beginning of the twentieth century and gazed into the future with understanding. Another received renewed public respect and honor. Still another coped with the long illness of a spouse only to become mentally infirm.

The person who did not live to see the 1880s was John Swaim. The prominent minister died on November 18, 1875, and his family faithfully carried his body home to Newark for burial. Appropriate to a person of his stature, he received three separate obituaries—the longest credited him for being "largely" responsible for the "influx of tourists" in Florida.[1] Swaim's widow, Catherine, lived on for more than a decade, but this was not a blessing since during this time she laid all of her children to rest. Consumption, which had killed her daughter in 1862, spread to other family members, taking from her both Matthias in 1879 and his brother Jacob soon afterwards. The remaining son, Thomas, died of Bright's disease in October 1884.

After Catherine's death, her grandson Wilbur sold the boardinghouse and threw "box after box" of his grandfather's records "in the old well" on the back of the property. When asked about his family background in 1936, he emphasized connections to Alabama and ignored any links to New Jersey. Yet, curiously, he lived in a Yankee enclave in South Jacksonville and built a home within a stone's throw from the Reeds.

While Thomas Swaim lay dying of Bright's disease, the same affliction visited Calvin Stowe. Writing a friend in 1884, Harriet Beecher Stowe described her husband as "no longer able to walk out, can do only a little reading and no writing."[2] As this happened, Harriet Beecher Stowe ended their trips to Mandarin and devoted her energy to an ailing "rabbi," as she affectionately called him. Even though family members said "he longed for death" as early as February 1885, it did not come until August 6, 1886.[3] Mrs. Stowe herself went into decline in 1889, and by 1890 a daughter described her as having the mind of a "child of two or three years." She died on July 1, 1896.[4]

As Calvin Stowe's health deteriorated, other tragedies befell the Beechers, especially Stowe's youngest half brother, James. After military service, he returned to the ministry. While James was serving as pastor of the First Congregation Church of Poughkeepsie, Henry Ward Beecher was charged with adultery. Shortly before Henry's famous trial, James went to his brother's home. The meeting did not go as James wished, and the younger man returned to Poughkeepsie and locked himself in his study. After many days he emerged "a changed man." James's "sunny nature" gave way to "curt sadness."[5] After this unsettling transformation his church offered Beecher a vacation but he resigned instead.

After leaving Poughkeepsie in 1876, James headed into the mountains. With the completion of a forest cottage, his wife and daughter joined him. Over the next decade they lived quietly. A newspaper later said, "During his entire residence he was always ready to help the poor with hands and money."[6] While Henry Ward's assistant pastor described James as being "insane for many years," the actual situation may not have been so simple.[7] The writer Ned Buntline, also known as Colonel Judson, befriended Beecher and reached a very different conclusion: James was a "genius."[8] Unfortunately, rejecting social prominence and living a simple Christian life did not solve Beecher's problems. Suffering from melancholia and perhaps post-traumatic stress disorder, the result of combat during the Civil War, he took the water-cure. For some unknown reason he was given access to firearms, and he used a gun to commit suicide on August 25, 1886. His wife, Frankie Beecher, remarried and a decade later published a touching account of their wartime experiences in the South.[9]

With Calvin Stowe's illness, Charles Beecher left Florida. Physically and mentally robust, he accepted the pastorate of a Presbyterian church in Wysox, Pennsylvania. After working for another eight years, he retired in 1893 and moved to a daughter's home in Georgetown, Massachusetts. In the years that followed, Beecher read widely in politics, science, and literature. As socialism and evolution were introduced, he quickly became aware of their theological implications. Reducing both to their basic tenets, he became alarmed.

Socialism, to him, rested upon principles that were accurate yet flawed. Beecher concurred with the notion that "society is wrongly organized" since it is founded upon selfishness. Because of its nature, "society must be reorganized in accordance with benevolence."[10] The belief that society must be reformed created no difficulties with Beecher: "it was something that the Bible teaches everywhere."[11] The problem came when socialists overemphasized external causes. Too many of them believed that the young entered "life pure" and became "corrupted by the system into which it came."[12] By changing an unjust economic order, then, according to the socialists, an earthly utopia could be had.

Such a thought clashed with the beliefs for which Beecher had been tried as a heretic. To him, souls, or spirits, came to the earth because of their imperfections. In the process of living, they could be improved and ultimately reconciled to God. Many human difficulties arose from internal frailties, weaknesses that could be modified. Charles wrote, "Moral evil is always the abuse of something good, either by excess or defect. It is excessive self-indulgence, or self-pleasing or selfishness. Pride is an excess of a good quality; so is ambition; so is avarice, and every other lust."[13] How a person lived made an enormous difference, and one life helped to shape the next. Because of its failure to consider internal causes and the need for individual responsibility, Beecher believed that socialism was too flawed for its principles to achieve utopia.

Beecher was likewise uncomfortable with the theological implications of evolution. Evolution, to him, argued that we emerged from "protoplasm or primordial germ." Charles wrote, "Rather than being a fallen race, we were an emerging one."[14] Much like socialism, it attributed our development to external causes. If we were shaped and molded by the environment, as evolution suggested, what became of our own responsibility for our sins?

As the twentieth century neared, challenges to Christianity arose in literature and the arts. Beecher claimed that the best-educated learned from non-Christian sources: "What trace of Trinitarianism is there in Browning, Matthew Arnold, George Eliot, Carlyle, Emerson, Hawthorne, Whitman, Lowell, Holmes, Rudyard Kipling, Hardy, Henry James, Mill, Spencer, Darwin, and a score of others who do the modern man's thinking?"[15] Trends within politics, science, and art assaulted Christianity from all sides. Looking ahead to the new century, Beecher expected the worst to happen. As a consequence, he conducted his own analysis of the book of Revelation, fully anticipating the end of time. At the age of eighty, he published his thoughts in a book, *Patmos: Or, The Unveiling*. In spite of the challenges, he concluded that the faith would prevail. Christ would stand again; the second coming would happen. Comforted by these thoughts, Charles died on April 21, 1900.

While Charles worked industriously on his farm and restarted his career as a minister, the Reeds led active lives. With the deaths of two sons, Chloe Merrick Reed recommitted herself to social causes. She joined Martha Reed Mitchell in the association that managed St. Luke's Hospital. During 1882 to 1884 she served as vice president and from 1885 to 1886 as its treasurer.[16] Not limited by the narrowness of denominations, she supported worthy causes—a Catholic orphanage, a fledgling Methodist church in South Jacksonville, and charities that won the goodwill of members of the Jewish community.

In 1888, Harrison Reed was tempted by wealth yet again. Alexander Mitchell had died, and Martha appeared to be in poor health. Since Mitchell could no longer direct her affairs in Florida, Reed wrote her son U.S. Senator John Mitchell seeking permission to help. He offered to take charge and Chloe could supervise her care. Or, as an alternative, he could work with David Mitchell, who seemed to be capable. What Reed did not tell the senator was that Martha Mitchell had financed a business venture with one of Reed's older sons. When the deal went sour, she ended the financing. Rather than dying or even remaining feeble, Martha Mitchell recovered. Learning of her brother's letters, she suspected the worst. In yet another letter to the senator, Reed "admitted that Chloe had not been told the entire truth." "I do not even now," he declared, "let my good wife know all of the necessities of this dreadful case."[17] Nothing Harrison did or said reduced Mitchell's anger, and she exiled the Reeds from Villa Alexandria. This event forced Chloe Merrick Reed to leave the hospital association. As her husband put it, "She has been compelled to resign to protect its interests."[18]

This disaster came before unexpected good news. Reed's political connections bore fruit, and he was appointed postmaster for Tallahassee. This enabled him to supplement his farming income with a federal salary, providing economic stability. Being in public office led to renewed contacts with African Americans. Times had changed and moderate Democrats gave way to racists bent on political domination. The region east of Tallahassee became a center of violence. Racists intimidated witnesses, violated elections laws, and drove Yankees from their property. When an African American testified in court about election irregularities, he was promptly murdered. Looking for help, one black man called on Reed so often at a hotel that complaints from guests appeared in the newspaper. Rather than remaining silent, the former governor turned to the northern press.

As Reed described the situation in the *Milwaukee Sentinel*, a senator from Wisconsin suggested the use of federal force to insure honest elections in the South. This proposal elicited two very different reactions—

one from the *Sentinel* itself and the other from Reed. The newspaper opposed the notion that the "central government receive the votes, count them, and declare the results."[19] While the authors of this proposal had "good motives," they could not prevent the violence or the intimidation: "We think that in the present phase of civilization in states like Mississippi and parts of Louisiana, with the intense prejudice of the white race; their determination that none but Democrats shall be elected; their readiness to employ violence; and the unorganized condition and timidity of Negroes, such a law would be wholly ineffective."[20]

Reed, on the other hand, applauded the senator's efforts—"God bless him"—and attacked the *Sentinel:* "The state governments in the South have one and all nullified the civil rights guaranteed by the constitution."[21] What then is more dangerous? Reed said that federal government had a choice: "enforce respect for its laws" or watch their violent subversion.[22] By failing to help the heroic few who resisted tyranny, the *Sentinel* engaged in "cowardice." The situation in Florida was complicated by a racist press, a claim Reed supported with a copy of the *Monticello Tribune.* Rather than supporting law enforcement, the editor of the *Tribune* accused federal officials of trying to "humiliate our people." Then the newspaper counseled readers to defy marshals: "We would see [the blood of the] first born splattered on the threshold of every home. Turn every house into an arsenal and every farm into a camp ground."[23]

When Republicans in Congress failed to act, oppression reached new heights. The governor responded to the election of Republicans to local offices in Jacksonville by removing them and appointing Democrats. When the same disgraceful and illegal behavior happened in other towns, the state supreme court stood shamefully idle. With the subsequent murder of a U.S. deputy marshal, Reed observed that federal officials were not protected. Not even a district judge could safely "execute the laws against fraud or conspiracy or violence." The failure of federal authorities to respond worsened the situation, "compounded by the tone of the press." In a series of four articles between early November 1889, and February 22, 1890, Reed pushed the case for federal help: "The culmination is now reached and either patriotism and loyalty must succumb to local despotism or the federal government must assert its authority and protect the civil rights guaranteed by the constitution."[24]

As Harrison struggled and lost, Chloe Merrick Reed received a series of honors. In 1890 the state made plans to participate in the 1893 World's Fair in Chicago. A committee selected four commissioners, two men and two women, to be leaders for this event. Each of these people were, in turn, backed by an alternate. The committee honored Chloe Merrick Reed by naming her as one of the alternates and circulated her photo with the state's promotional materials. In the same period, the animosity between Martha Mitchell and the Reeds abated enough for the hospital association to name Chloe an honorary director. Not content with the recognition in health care, the AME church honored her contributions to African American education by inviting her to its convention in February 1896. It thrilled her to see one of her former pupils, a bishop, "occupying the highest position in his church."[25]

The next honor for Chloe Merrick Reed came posthumously. In the summer of 1897, she collapsed, lived for four or five weeks after a stroke, and died on August 5. At the time, her family again had limited resources, having lost their splendid orange grove in the great freeze. Rather than letting this situation diminish the funeral, the Jewish community rushed to the family's assistance. Chloe's grandson recalled, "Mr. Jake Cohen was so grateful to her for her kindness in bringing understanding among the citizens of Jacksonville that he insisted on outfitting her in fine arrayment for her burial."[26] Relatives buried Chloe Merrick Reed in clothing worthy of a state funeral, given in an outpouring of love and respect. In contrast to her many friends, Harrison Reed reacted without emotion, showing little grief at the funeral. It was thought that he was so near death that he would be with Mrs. Reed within weeks.

At the age of eighty-four and living in a hostile era, Reed turned to one remaining task. Not trusting the press either in the North or in Florida, he wrote his own obituary and gave it to Charles Kinne. The process took

Reed back to his youth. As he started writing, Kinne believed, "the strength of earlier years" returned and his handwriting became "clear and legible."[27] Reed's thoughts went to his parents and his birth at Littleton, Massachusetts, on August 26, 1813. When he was a child, the family moved to Vermont, the place of his mother's birth. In Rutland, Harrison attended a local academy until he was sixteen and became an apprentice in the firm that printed a local newspaper.

Leaving the publishing business in the early 1830s, he worked in a store in Troy, New York. This background enabled him to open his own mercantile concern in Milwaukee, then a "trading post." When the nation's economy faltered in 1837, Reed lost his business. Financially ruined, he and his brothers turned to homesteading on government land. This decision was followed rapidly by an opportunity. Joining the *Milwaukee Sentinel* as a "practical printer, he became its publisher and editor." Reed claimed to have laid the "foundation for the first Whig newspaper in the territory west of Lake Michigan, and which is today, one of the most important Republican newspapers of the northwest."[28]

After five years at the *Sentinel*, Reed joined newspapers in Madison and then Neenah, where he developed the town, before returning to Madison. The last move occurred so that his children could attend the state university. At the start of the Civil War, Reed's only daughter died of diphtheria, and "his wife was an invalid requiring immediate removal to a warmer climate."[29] Responding to her needs, he used his political connections to get a position as "assistant secretary for the House of Representatives." When this appointment went astray, he obtained a post in Fernandina as a tax commissioner. In spite of Reed's hopes, these efforts came too late, and his first wife died in October 1862.

In writing about his marriage to Chloe Merrick, he noted her accomplishments. To this he added her service with the World's Fair and the observation that she had died on "the eve of their silver wedding anniversary."[30] At this point Reed chose only to make a few comments about his years as governor. He wanted Floridians to know that his successor had been elected "without a disturbance at a single poll" and that he had improved the state's financial credit. Before ending his obituary, Reed mentioned the *Semi-Tropical*. He described it as a "most honorable achievement."[31]

Since Reed offered few words about his administration, Charles Kinne added his own observations, something he was eminently qualified to do. Chloe's nephew, Emma and Ansel's son, had served as the governor's personal secretary in Tallahassee.

Charles described Reed as "one of the most abused men in the state."[32] Traditional southerners, still suffering from the costs of the Civil War, regarded him as an "alien and an enemy." At the same time he was vehemently opposed by many Republicans. According to Kinne, "At least one third, and a very powerful one third, did all in their power to hinder him."[33] Among them were "knaves and adventurers" ready to prey upon the people. Finding their plans obstructed, they tortured Reed with impeachment. All of these experiences took a dreadful toll on the governor. His "pleasant and kindly face" became marred by wrinkles, "the results of mental strife and unsatisfactory memories."

In spite of the politics of the Reconstruction, Kinne wanted Reed to be remembered as a fiscal and social conservative: "He adopted the middle course against those who [wanted] a black man's government and those who desired a white man's government."[34] By following this difficult road, Reed supposedly minimized violence. In financial affairs, the governor sought to restore the state's credit. To achieve this result, he proposed new taxes. Yet he wanted this done fairly. As a consequence, Reed sought a "state board to equalize the tax among counties so that no injustice was done by under or over assessment."[35]

Although Kinne mentioned that the governor refused to use "martial law" in office, this was not, in fact, an achievement to boast of, because that refusal led to KKK violence in several counties. While Reed sought federal force in the 1890s, he had, himself, declined to use state troops to uphold civil rights in the Reconstruction.

To everyone's surprise, the ancient Yankee did not die in 1897. Reed recovered and lived until May 25, 1899. In this period he talked constantly of "Mrs. Reed's life and companionship."[36]

Legacy

The story of the origins of modern Florida affirms the wisdom of mature adults. In an era of poor sanitation, limited knowledge of communicable diseases, and dangerous medical practices, none of our reformers was young. In August 1864 John Swaim turned fifty-eight before he first saw the state; Harriet Beecher Stowe was fifty-five when she came in March 1867; Charles Beecher was fifty-one; and Harrison Reed was almost fifty in 1862. At thirty, Chloe Merrick, the youngest of the group, was vigorous, energetic, and attractive. Yet a woman of thirty in the 1860s would have been regarded as a confirmed spinster long past the age of marriage.

Among the reformers who helped give birth to modern Florida, the dream can be traced to the oldest of the group and perhaps the most ill. Few people in the North would have been surprised had John Swaim come to Florida and died quickly. But the combination of age and the prospect of a limited life shaped Swaim's desire to act. Rather than being passive, or wondering if individual effort made a difference, Swaim acted—a trait shared with his Yankee forebears. With his plan to seize Florida in mind, he set out to attract tourists. An important newspaper published and reprinted his articles, multiplying their effect. Still others joined him in writing to the *Sentinel of Freedom*, and by 1877 over sixty different articles appeared.[1]

Harriet Beecher Stowe, Harrison Reed, and Eunice Bullard Beecher adopted Swaim's strategy. The Beechers enhanced his efforts with two books and over forty articles about the state, most of them in the widely circulated *Christian Union*. To this literature Harrison Reed added over thirty issues of the *Semi-Tropical* and a state office to publicize Florida. Because tourists and the infirm responded, hotel construction in Jacksonville continued during the depression of the 1870s. When Henry Flagler began thinking about creating luxury hotels in St. Augustine, gentlemen of his social class already frequented the resort. He purchased the railroad from Tocoi from William Astor.[2]

To achieve the ambitious goal of making Florida a modern state required more than tourism, and every family that helped give it birth engaged in innovative farming. Advice in *Palmetto-Leaves* and the *Semi-Tropical* not only encouraged Florida's agricultural development but also enhanced the likelihood of success for newcomers. Because of tourism and new residents, Stowe reported a very important fact in 1877: "About all of the money circulating in the state comes from northern immigrants and visitors."[3] The presence of these resources transformed property values. In 1889 Reed noted a marked difference between the Jacksonville area and the region near Tallahassee where tourists seldom went: "East and south Florida are within control of northern capital and its lands have appreciated in value to five and ten times the price of lands in middle Florida."[4] This increase occurred in spite of the fact that better soil and larger farms were in middle Florida.

As property values increased, money became available for education. New citizens opened schools in county systems created by legislation signed by Harrison Reed. Not content with the governor's contribution, Chloe Merrick Reed and Charles Beecher sought participation from a broad range of citizens, reducing objections to public schools. Their extraordinary success led to a rapid growth in enrollments and popular support for school financing. When Democrats reduced funding in 1879, the public outcry forced a rapid retreat.

The social and political future of modern Florida required an educated public. With this in mind, Charles Beecher formed a bipartisan governing board for the state's new agricultural college, and the Swaims helped give birth to both Cookman Institute and Duval High School. These schools continued into the 1920s, when Cookman was merged with Mary McCloud Bethune's school at Daytona Beach to form Bethune-Cookman College. The success of Matthias Swaim's school and the continuing demand for secondary education required the creation of three new high schools as its replacement.

Beyond these accomplishments, Florida's social reformers left other legacies. Harriet Beecher Stowe herself believed that *Uncle Tom's Cabin* had been written with divine participation. As a response to a loving God, the Stowes, Swaims, and Reeds founded churches. John Sanford Swaim organized two of them—Zion Methodist Episcopal Church, which still exists as Ebenezer United Methodist Church, and Trinity Methodist Episcopal Church, which became Snyder Memorial, serving as a part of the United Methodist Church until the early 1990s. The Reeds, together with John Swaim's grandson, opened Grace Methodist Episcopal Church, and it exists today as Swaim Memorial.

The successes of the Beechers, Swaims, and Reeds required meaningful participation of African Americans. Quick to seize upon economic and educational opportunities, blacks flocked to Jacksonville. As a result they formed a majority of the citizenry for decades. In public affairs they remained a force within the state long after the Reconstruction. The Beechers, Swaims, and Reeds did not create modern Florida by themselves but rather were joined in their endeavors by thousands of eager Floridians.

When the origin of modern Florida is attributed to its real sources, the history of the state becomes richer and far more relevant. Henry Flagler and others called robber barons didn't start modern Florida, they only expanded it. Flagler discovered a winner and thought enough of it to invest millions. As he did, he became a generous and humane individual—no longer the Henry Flagler who came to a few hardships in 1878 and callously let his wife die.

This part of the South, modern Florida, attracted creative Yankees. Rejoicing with a renewed purpose for living—Charles Beecher's recovery was dramatic—they gave lovingly to the state, enriching its schools, churches, and political life. Unfortunately, their dream of a northern state in southern climes—one characterized by social, racial, and religious reforms—was not embraced by the next generation of leaders.

Harriet Beecher Stowe, commenting on her bird, Phoebus, a resident in her Mandarin home, reported: "This morning being Sunday, he called, Beecher! Beecher! Very Volubly. He evidently is a progressive bird and for aught we know may yet express himself on some of the questions of the day."[5] She and others came to the South and did far more than comment on the issues of the day. These Yankees came as strangers but are strangers no more. Their contributions to the development of Florida can be celebrated in any age.

NOTES

Preface

1. Quoted in Charles Edward Stowe, *Life of Harriet Beecher Stowe*, 410.
2. Cash, *Story of Florida*, 484.
3. Ibid.
4. Dovell, *Florida: Historic, Dramatic, Contemporary*, 629.
5. Ibid.
6. Graham, *The Awakening of St. Augustine*, 167.

Chapter 1

1. CU, May 8, 1872.
2. Harriet Beecher Stowe to George Beecher, quoted in Hedrick, *Harriet Beecher Stowe*, 64.
3. Hedrick, *Harriet Beecher Stowe*, 143–57.
4. Ibid., 157.
5. Ibid., 342.
6. The statistical description of tourism appears in James R. Ward, *Old Hickory's Town*, 158. References to hotels can be found in T. Frederick Davis, *History of Jacksonville, Florida, and Vicinity, 1513 to 1924*, 486. Lanier's comments were published in the *Times-Union* (Jacksonville), January 30, 1916.

For over a century it has been possible to identify more than one Florida. On the clay hills east and west of Tallahassee stood cotton plantations. Some of them were owned by relatives of Thomas Jefferson and Napoleon Bonaparte, and, like such farms in Georgia and Alabama, they were dependent upon slavery. More than one hundred miles to the east rested remnants of colonial development. In St. Augustine were buildings from Spanish periods—Fort San Marco, a small cathedral, and numerous homes—and a population that had stayed since the British occupation. Between these regions, and stretching off to the south, were miles of sandy soil with isolated farms breaking a sea of pines and palmettos. Along this frontier were families raising corn, cattle, and hogs. These people supplemented incomes by hunting and later by logging. In juxtaposition to these Floridas stood hotels that attracted northern tourists, farms where citrus and winter crops flourished, and communities seeking the retired or ill as residents.

In a simplified fashion there were four Floridas: one that resembled the plantation "Old South," another connected by history and culture to "Colonial Spanish," a third that could be characterized as "Rural Frontier," and the last that could be labeled "Modern Florida."

Our understanding of the origins of the four Floridas is uneven. Writers and historians have found certain topics more appealing than others. Conquistadors, British trading companies, aristocratic planters, and native American leaders have been the subjects of books and numerous articles. Even the "Rural Frontier," celebrated in novels such as *The Yearling*, is the topic of recent historical works. Yet the origins of modern Florida are less understood.

For a book about rural life, see Canter Brown, *Florida's Peace River Frontier.* For information on the origin of modern Florida, see the following articles: John T. Foster, Jr., Herbert B. Whitmer, Jr., and Sarah Whitmer Foster, "Tourism Was Not the Only Purpose: Jacksonville Republicans and Newark's *Sentinel of Freedom*"; Foster and Foster, "John Sanford Swaim: A Life at the Beginning of Modern Florida"; Foster and Foster, "The Last Shall Be First: Northern Methodists in Reconstruction Jacksonville"; Foster and Foster, "Chloe Merrick Reed: Freedom's First Lady"; and Foster and Foster, "Aid Societies Were Not Alike: Northern Teachers in Post–Civil War Florida."

7. NSF, June 1, 1875. See also Foster and Foster, "St. Augustine Visit in 1875," *Florida Living*, 12–13.

8. Ibid.

9. CU, May 13, 1873; Stowe, *Palmetto-Leaves*, 262.

10. See Stowe, *Uncle Tom's Cabin*, 368.

11. References to Legree are found on page 174 in Lyman Beecher Stowe's *Saints, Sinners, and Beechers*: "Charles Beecher actually met the Legree of real life" and recorded his remarks by a kind of "shorthand." "Legree was drawn from life more exactly than any other character" (in *Uncle Tom's Cabin*).

Chapter 2

1. SDS, December 28, 1891; April 26, 1985.

2. Ibid, SJ, August 2, 1856.

3. Gurko, *The Ladies of Seneca Falls*, 100; SDS, September 6, 1852.

4. Luther Lee, *Woman's Right to Preach the Gospel*, 5.

5. Gurko, *The Ladies of Seneca Falls*, 134.

6. Foster and Foster, "Aid Societies Were Not Alike," 311; *Syracuse Herald*, November 19, 1922.

7. Foster and Foster, "Chloe Merrick Reed," 282; *New York Daily Tribune*, July 25, 1851.

8. *New York Daily Tribune*, October 6, 1851; *True Wesleyan* (New York), June 14, 1851.

9. *Syracuse Herald*, October 1, 1899; see also Foster and Foster, "Chloe Merrick Reed," 282.

10. *Syracuse Herald*, October 1, 1899.

11. Ibid.; Foster and Foster, "Chloe Merrick Reed," 282.

12. SDS, April 19, 1884.

13. "Strict injunctions were given by Gerrit Smith and others not to intentionally injure the police." *Syracuse Herald*, October 1, 1899; see also Foster and Foster, "Chloe Merrick Reed," 283.

14. NF, June 1866, 161–62.

15. Ibid.

16. Ibid.

17. SDS, December 23, 1862.

18. (Boston) *Liberator*, December 12, 1862.

19. Quoted in SDS, March 4, 1863; Foster and Foster, "Chloe Merrick Reed," 284.

20. SJ, April 15, 1864.

21. SDS, January 12, 1863; SJ, April 15, 1864.

22. SDS, March 4, 1863; SJ, May 20, 1863.

23. Quoted in Current, *Those Terrible Carpetbaggers*, 26.

24. Ibid.

25. Daniels, *Prince of Carpetbaggers*, 83–84.

26. Ibid.

27. Quoted ibid, 84.

28. SJ, April 15, 1864.

29. Ibid.

30. Ibid., November 12, 1863.

31. SDS, September 16, 1863.

32. SJ, September 4, 1863.

33. Ibid.

34. Ibid., December 24, 1863.

35. NF, June 1866, 173.

36. Schwartz, *A Woman Doctor's Civil War*, 99.

37. NF, June 1866, 173.

38. SJ, April 22, 1865; NF, June 1865, 181.

39. Futch, "Salmon P. Chase and Civil War Politics in Florida," 163.

40. Ibid.

41. Quoted in Current, *Those Terrible Carpetbaggers*, 27.

42. Foster and Foster, "Aid Societies Were Not Alike," 315–16; *New York Tribune*, May 22, 25, 1865.

43. NF, January 1866, 3; April 1866, 115.

44. Ibid.

45. Engs, *Freedom's First Generation*, 143–44.

46. Quoted ibid.

47. Foster and Foster, "Aid Societies Were Not Alike," 314.

48. Engs, *Freedom's First Generation*, 145.

49. Foster and Foster, "Aid Societies Were Not Alike," 314.

50. SJ, June 8, 1865.

51. Ibid.

52. Ibid.

53. Ibid.

54. Quoted in Schuckers, *The Life and Public Services of Salmon Portland Chase*, 523.

55. SJ, June 8, 1865.

Chapter 3

1. *Minutes of the Newark Conference*, 1876, 42; see also Foster and Foster, "John Sanford Swaim: A Life," 231.

2. *Minutes of the Newark Conference*, 42.

3. Ibid.; Foster and Foster, "The Last Shall Be First," 268.

4. *The New Jersey Conference Memorial*, 511–12.

5. Foster and Foster, "The Last Shall Be First," 270.

6. Lyman Beecher Stowe, *Saints, Sinners, and Beechers*, 384–85.

7. Ibid., 385.

8. Ibid.

9. Perkins, "Two Years with a Colored Regiment," 535.

10. James C. Beecher to Frankie Johnson, March 11, 1864, Harriet Beecher Stowe Center.

11. Ibid.

12. Perkins, "Two Years with a Colored Regiment," 534.

13. James C. Beecher to Frankie Beecher, August 1, 1864, Harriet Beecher Stowe Center.

14. Perkins, "Two Years with a Colored Regiment," 537.

15. Silliman, *A New Canaan Private in the Civil War*, 77–78.

16. Ibid.

17. Ibid.

18. Ibid.; *The New Jersey Conference Memorial*, 511.

19. Silliman, *A New Canaan Private in the Civil War*, 81.

20. Perkins, "Two Years with a Colored Regiment," 537.

21. Ibid.

22. Ibid., 538.

23. Ibid., 539.

24. Hedrick, *Harriet Beecher Stowe*, 305.

25. *Christian Advocate* (New York), June 8, 1865.

26. Ibid.

27. Williams, "A Century of Compromise," 158.

28. Ibid.

29. Morrow, *Northern Methodism and Reconstruction*, 48–49.

30. Ibid., 54.

31. Foster and Foster, "The Last Shall Be First," 269–70; diary of John Swaim, collection of the authors, May 14, June 4, 1866, and January 2, 1867.

32. NDA, May 30, 1865.

33. Ibid.

34. Ibid.

35. NSF, January 7, 1868.

36. Sheats, "Twenty-Fifth Annual Report," 6–9.

37. *Minutes of the Newark Conference of the Methodist Episcopal Church, 1876* , 52.

38. NSF, April 22, 1865.

39. Ibid.

40. NDA, May 2, 1865.

41. Ibid.

42. Ibid.

43. NDA, May 30, 1865.

44. Brown, *Ossian Bingley Hart*, 44.

Chapter 4

1. NF, June 1865, 182.

2. Ibid.

3. Simpson, Graf, and Muldown, *Advice after Appomattox*, 3–16, 35.

4. A. Mot to S. P. Chase, June 30, 1865, Salmon P. Chase Papers, Library of Congress.

5. Brown, *Florida's Black Public Officials*, 1.

6. Foster and Foster, "Aid Societies Were Not Alike," 321–22.

7. A. E. Kinne to T. W. Osborn, January 2, 1866, BRFAL.

8. Foster and Foster, "Aid Societies Were Not Alike," 322; F. G. Shaw to O. O. Howard, April 18, 1866, Charles Beecher Letters, Special Collections, Bowdoin College Library, Brunswick, Maine.

9. NF, April 1866, 115; December 1865, 346.

10. NF, April 1866, 114–15.

11. Diary of John S. Swaim, collection of the authors, January 18–June 4, 1866.

12. NF, December 1865, 346.

13. *American Freedman*, April 1868, 192.

14. Ibid.

15. T. W. Osborn to H. H. Moore, April 19, 1866; Moore to Osborn, April 23, 1866, BRFAL.

16. Quoted in Brown, *Florida's Black Public Officials*, 3.

17. Ibid., 2–6.

18. *American Freedman*, April 1869, 4, 5, 11.

19. ST, August 1877.

20. NDA, August 29, 1865.

21. Ibid.

22. Ibid.

23. Ibid.

24. Ibid.

25. Ibid., March 21, 1866.

26. Ibid.

27. Ibid., March 2, 1866.

28. Ibid.

29. Ibid., March 21, 1866.

30. Ibid.

31. Quoted in Richardson, "A Northerner Reports on Florida," 389.

32. Ibid., 382–83, 390.

33. Ibid., 382.

34. Ibid.

35. Ibid., 383.

36. Ibid., 390.

37. Foster and Foster, "The Last Shall Be First," 272–73.

38. Diary of John Swaim, November 9, 1866.

39. Ibid., May 22 and 23, June 15, 1866.

40. Ibid.

41. Foster and Foster, "John Sanford Swaim: A Life," 234.

42. *Christian Advocate* (New York), November 15, 1866.

43. Ibid.

44. NSF, November 26, 1867.

45. Quoted in Simpson, Graf, and Muldown, *Advice after Appomattox*, 15.

46. Ibid.

47. Diary of John Swaim, March 21, 1866.

48. Brown, *Ossian Bingley Hart*, 193.

49. Ibid., 192, 297.

50. Harriet Beecher Stowe, "Our Florida Plantation," 649.

51. Hedrick, *Harriet Beecher Stowe*, 174–85.

52. SJ, October 1, 1866.

Chapter 5

1. Charles Beecher's diary for the March 1867 trip to Florida is a part of the Harriet Beecher Stowe Collection, Stowe-Day Library (hereafter, Stowe Papers). See entries for March 12–14.

2. Quoted in Hedrick, *Harriet Beecher Stowe*, 328.

3. Charles Edward Stowe, *Life of Harriet Beecher Stowe*, 400.

4. Quoted in Hedrick, *Harriet Beecher Stowe*, 220; References to Legree can be found on page 174 in Lyman Beecher Stowe, *Saints, Sinners, and Beechers*, 4.

5. Diary of Charles Beecher, March 11.

6. Ibid., March 12–14.

7. Ibid.

8. Graff, *Mandarin on the St. Johns*, 49.

9. NSF, March 19, 1873; April 23, 1873; for references to Christopher Spencer Foote, see Graff, *Mandarin on the St. Johns*, 47.

10. H. B. Stowe to "Dear Sir," n. d. (*c.* 1868 to 1870), Stowe Papers.

11. H. B. Stowe to Charles Beecher, quoted in Charles Edward Stowe, *Life of Harriet Beecher Stowe*, 401.

12. H. B. Stowe to Calvin Stowe, April 7, 1867, Stowe Papers; the change in land purchase is mentioned in Graff, *Mandarin on the St. Johns*, 45.

13. For a discussion of the plight of women writers, see Hedrick, *Harriet Beecher Stowe*, 329–52.

14. Quoted ibid., 349.

15. Ibid., 354–73.

16. Quoted ibid., 363.

17. Quoted ibid., 363, 369.

18. Ibid., 370.

19. NSF, January 7, 1868.

20. Harriet Beecher Stowe, "Villa Alexandria," 448–51.

21. Charles Stowe, *Life of Harriet Beecher Stowe*, 339; (Boston) *Liberator,* September 18, 1863, offered the opinion that the church body's decision was an "act of conspiracy" that set out to "entrap" him; also see the *Boston Journal,* July 23, 1863; Hull, *Georgetown: Story of One Hundred Years,* 19–20.

22. Ibid.

23. Brief accounts of Charles Beecher's life appear in a number of works: Johnson, *Dictionary of American Biography,* 11, 126–27; Lyman Beecher Stowe, *Saints, Sinners, and Beechers,* 223–24, 336–43; and Rugoff, *The Beechers: An American Family in the Nineteenth Century,* 519–24. The sermon quotation comes from *Saints, Sinners,* 337.

24. Diary of Charles Beecher, March 6, 1867.

25. Ibid., March 17, 1867.

26. Charles Beecher to Sarah Beecher, November 9, 1869, Stowe Papers; Henry Ward Beecher commented on his brother's plight: "His oldest son was shot in the rebellion, hobbled back and was shot again, and then went into the regular army. On the border he was surrounded by Indians and killed, and the judgment day will have to search all over the plains for his bones. Now, my boy went through the war and came out with only a bruise. My brother Charles had two daughters. They went sailing on a lake in the very sight of his house and were drowned. Why is my brother thus dealt with, and not me?" (TWF, December 23, 1873).

27. Charles Beecher to Sarah Beecher, November 7, 1869; Charles Beecher to C. M. Beecher, November 10, 1869, Stowe Papers.

28. NSF, November 26, 1867.

29. Ibid., May 11, 1869.

30. Ibid., July 6, 1869, and September 28, 1869.

31. Ibid., February 1, 1870.

32. Davis, *History of Jacksonville*, 487–90.

33. NSF, August 25, 1868.

34. Ibid.

35. Ibid.

36. Ibid., March 2, 1869.

37. *Boston Daily Advertiser*, March 11, 1868.

38. Ibid.

39. Ibid.

40. NSF, July 7, 1868.

41. Ibid.

42. Ibid.

43. Ibid., September 29, 1868.

44. Foster, Whitmer, and Foster, "Tourism Was Not the Only Purpose," 319.

45. Quoted in Shofner, *Nor Is It Over Yet*, 264.

46. Foster and Foster, "The Last Shall Be First," 276–77.

47. Davis, *History of Jacksonville*, 491.

Chapter 6

1. The Reconstruction is an unfamiliar world to many Americans. An important overview can be seen in Eric Foner, *Reconstruction: America's Unfinished Revolution, 1863 –1877* .

2. Brown, *Ossian Bingley Hart*, 193.

3. Ibid., 192.

4. Ibid., 191; Brown, *Florida's Black Public Officials*, 3.

5. Brown, *Ossian Bingley Hart*, 192.

6. Quoted in Brown, *Florida's Black Public Officials*, 4.

7. Ibid., 5.

8. Ibid., 3.

9. FU, July 20, 1867.

10. Quoted in Brown, *Florida's Black Public Officials*, 10.

11. Ibid., 11.

12. Ibid., 13.

13. NSF, July 21, 1868.

14. Ibid.

15. Ibid.

16. Brown, *Florida's Black Public Officials*, 16.

17. Harrison Reed, "Governor's Message to the Legislature," *Assembly Journal: A Journal of the Proceedings of the State of Florida*, 43–44.

18. Ibid.

19. Ibid.

20. Rerick, *Memoirs of Florida*, 311, 313–14.

21. Ibid.

22. Ibid.

23. Ibid.

24. Brown, *Florida's Black Public Officials*, 17.

25. NSF, July 7, 1868.

26. Charles Beecher to Isabella Beecher Hooker, July 13, 1872, Stowe Papers.

27. Rerick, *Memoirs of Florida*, 314.

28. Ibid.

29. Current, *Those Terrible Carpetbaggers*, 90.

30. Foster and Foster, "Chloe Merrick Reed," 294.

31. SJ, August 11, 1869.

32. Ibid.

33. MS, September 15, 1869; reprinted in the *Examiner* (St. Augustine), October 2, 1869.

34. Ibid.

35. Ibid.

36. Johnson, *Dictionary of American Biography*, vol. 13, 39–40.

37. WPA Federal Writers' Project, "Interviews of Local Residents of Jacksonville (1936–1941)," Mollie Gibson LeNoir interview, Jacksonville Public Li-

brary. Descriptions of Villa Alexandria can also be found in interviews with David Mitchell and Mrs. Phena Hudnall Love.

38. Ibid.

39. Ibid., David Mitchell quoted in Phena Hudnall Love interview.

40. Ibid.

41. Ibid.

42. Diary of William C. Beecher, March 9, 1871, Beecher Family Papers, Yale University Library.

43. FU, February 11, 1869.

44. Eppes, *Through Some Eventful Years*, 316.

45. Ibid.

46. Ibid., 318.

47. Ibid.

Chapter 7

1. CU, May 21, 1870.

2. Ibid.

3. Ibid.

4. Ibid.

5. Ibid.

6. Rerick, *Memoirs of Florida*, 324.

7. Sheats, "Twenty-Fifth and Twenty-Sixth Annual Reports," 10–12.

8. *Tallahassee Sentinel*, March 25, 1871; Graff, *Mandarin on the St. Johns*, 58.

9. Charles Beecher to O. O. Howard, April 19, 1871, Special Collections, Bowdoin College Library, Brunswick, Maine.

10. Quoted in Lyman Beecher Stowe, *Saints, Sinners, and Beechers*, 341.

11. *Tallahassee Sentinel*, March 25, 1871.

12. References to the Freedmen's Bureau in Florida can be found in J. W. Alvord, *Fourth Semi-Annual Report*, 34.

13. Ibid., 37.

14. Cochran, *History of Public School Education*, 49.

15. Statistics for Chase's administration can be found in Sheats, "Twenty-Fifth and Twenty-Sixth Annual Reports," 9.

16. Daniels, *Prince of Carpetbaggers*, 252.

17. Charles Beecher, "Supplementary Report to Governor O. B. Hart," 42.

18. Sheats, "Twenty-Fifth and Twenty-Sixth Annual Reports," 14.

19. The growth in schools under Charles Beecher and Chloe Reed can be found in Sheats, "Twenty-Fifth and Twenty-Sixth Annual Reports," Appendix A.

20. Ibid., 171.

21. References to the high rate of literacy in Florida are in Kingman, *Neither Dies nor Surrenders: A History of the Republican Party in Florida*, 56.

22. Charles Beecher, "Report of the Superintendent of Public Instruction: For the Year Ending September 30, 1871," 59.

23. Ibid.

24. Cochran, *History of Public School Education*, 69.

25. Charles Beecher, "Report ... 1871," 58–59; for an extensive account of the history of the agricultural college, see Proctor, "The University of Florida: Its Early Years," 194–213.

26. Charles Beecher, "Report . . . 1871," 60.

27. Cochran, *History of Public School Education*, 69, 61.

28. *Christian Advocate* (New York), August 1, 1872; Foster and Foster, "The Last Shall Be First," 277.

29. Stowell, *Methodist Adventures in Negro Education*, 78.

30. *Christian Advocate* (New York), March 2, 1876.

31. Bush, *The History of Education in Florida*, 26.

32. Scott, *The Education of Black People in Florida*, 4.

33. Harshorn, *An Era of Progress and Promise*, 183.

34. *New South* (Jacksonville), September 30, 1874.

35. FU, October 3, 1876.

36. Bush, *The History of Education*, 30.

37. Foster and Foster, "The Last Shall Be First," 279.

38. This quote is from Rerick, *Memoirs of Florida*, 317. For a discussion of Littlefield's activities in North Carolina, see Daniels, *Prince of Carpetbaggers;* Canter Brown, Jr.'s, account of the politics of the period offers considerable insight; see his "Carpetbagger Intrigues," 275–301.

39. Quoted in Brown, "Carpetbagger Intrigues," 281.

40. Rerick, *Memoirs of Florida*, 316–17.

41. Ibid.

42. Brown, "Carpetbagger Intrigues," 282–83.

43. *Savannah Daily Republican*, February 14, 1872.

44. Brown, "Carpetbagger Intrigues," 286, 289.

45. Ibid., 286.

46. *Tallahassee Sentinel*, April 20, 1872.

47. Quoted in Brown, "Carpetbagger Intrigues," 287.

48. Ibid., 290.

49. Ibid., 291.

50. Charles Beecher to I. B. Hooker, July 13, 1872, Stowe Papers.

51. Brown, "Carpetbagger Intrigues," 296.
52. Ibid., 298.
53. Quoted ibid.
54. Ibid., 300.

Chapter 8

1. Hedrick, *Harriet Beecher Stowe*, 371.
2. CU, February 7, 1872.
3. CU, May 7, 1870; for the entire series, see the *Christian Union*, May 7, 21, 1870; February 7, 14, 21, 28, March, 13, 20, 27, April, 3, 10, 24, May 15, 22, 29, June 5, 19, and August 28, 1872.
4. CU, May 7, 1870.
5. Ibid.
6. Ibid.
7. Ibid., May 29, 1872.
8. Ibid.
9. Ibid.
10. Rerick, *Memoirs of Florida*, 325.
11. CU, February 14, 1872.
12. Ibid.
13. Ibid., February 26, 1873.
14. Ibid., June 14, 1872.
15. Ibid.
16. Ibid.
17. Ibid., May 8, 1872, May 22, 1872.
18. Ibid., Dec. 8, 1875.
19. Ibid.
20. Ibid., Feb. 21, 1872.
21. Ibid.
22. Harriet Beecher Stowe, *Palmetto-Leaves*, 317–18; CU, February 14, 1872.
23. Ibid.
24. Ibid.
25. Hedrick, *Harriet Beecher Stowe*, 389.
26. Quoted ibid.
27. Ibid.
28. CU, May 6, 1874; Davis, *History of Jacksonville*, 490.
29. Davis, *History of Jacksonville*, 491.
30. CU, May 14, 1873.

31. Ibid.
32. Ibid.
33. Ibid.
34. Ibid.
35. Ibid.
36. Ibid.
37. Ibid.
38. Ibid.
39. Ibid.
40. Ibid.
41. Ibid.
42. Ibid.
43. Ibid., May 6, 1874.
44. Ibid.
45. Ibid.
46. Ibid.
47. TWF, April 14, May 5, 1874; see also *Florida Union* (Jacksonville), March 24, 1874.
48. Foster, Whitmer, and Foster, "Tourism Was Not the Only Purpose," 318–24.
49. NSF, March 9, 1875.
50. Ibid.
51. FU, March 31, 1876; the early beginnings of the hospital are described in ST, March 1878, 148–49.
52. FU, March 31, 1876.
53. ST, August 1877, 449.
54. Ibid, 450.
55. Ibid.
56. Ibid.

Chapter 9

1. Because of his dealings with Littlefield, "Governor Reed is today a poor man" (*Syracuse Courier*, March 30, 1875). The foreclosure appears in TWF, April 4, 1876.
2. WPA Federal Writers' Project, "Interviews of Local Residents of Jacksonville (1934–1941)," Mollie Gibson LeNoir interview, Jacksonville Public Library.
3. Ibid.

4. The loss of two children is mentioned in Harrison M. Reed, Jr.'s, letter to Edward C. Williamson, March 15, 1953, Papers of the Florida Historical Society.

5. ST, October 1875, 128; Harrison Reed published reactions to his magazine in two articles, "Our Magazine," ST, October 1875, 128–29, and "Opinions of the Press," ST, December 1875, 256–57.

6. ST, October 1875, 128.

7. Ibid., 129.

8. Ibid.

9. Robinson, "A Lesson for Florida," ST, February 1876, 79–81.

10. Ibid.

11. Baldwin, "St. John's Bar," ST, June 1876, 321–40.

12. Charles Beecher, "Florida a Hundred Years Hence," ST, July 1877, 389–91, and "A Century Hence," ST, February 1878, 86–87.

13. Charles Beecher, "Florida a Hundred Years Hence," 390.

14. Ibid., 389.

15. Ibid.

16. Ibid.

17. Ibid., 391.

18. Diary of William C. Beecher, January to April, 1871.

19. Harriet Beecher Stowe, "Protect the Birds," ST, January 1877, 33–34.

20. Ibid, 33.

21. Ibid.

22. Ibid, 34.

23. ST, January 1877, 44.

24. Brown, *Florida's Black Public Officials*, ix.

25. CU, February 7, 1877.

26. Graff, *Mandarin on the St. Johns*, 68–69.

27. Harriet Beecher Stowe, "Education of Freedmen," 606-7.

28. Harriet Beecher Stowe, "Education of Freedmen, Part II," 93.

29. Ibid., 94.

30. Ibid.

31. Eunice Beecher, *Letters from Florida*, 26.

32. Ibid., 27.

33. Ibid.

34. Ibid., 81.

35. Ibid., 36.

36. TWF, January 13, 1880.

37. Ibid.

38. Ibid.

39. Ibid.

40. Covington, *Plant's Palace*, 49.

41. Chandler, *Henry Flagler: The Astonishing Life*, 87.

42. Ibid., 88.

43. Ibid.

44. Ibid., 94.

45. Quoted ibid.

46. Quoted in Akin, *Flagler: Rockefeller Partner*, 116.

47. Chandler, *Henry Flagler: The Astonishing Life*, 252.

48. Graff, *Mandarin on the St. Johns*, 71–72.

49. Ibid.

50. Chandler, *Henry Flagler: The Astonishing Life*, 144.

51. Ibid., 253.

52. WPA Federal Writers' Project, "Interviews of Local Residents of Jacksonville," David Mitchell interview, 49.

53. Ibid.

54. Ibid, 50.

55. Ibid.; for other descriptions of the fire, see Crooks, *Jacksonville: After the Fire*, 17-18.

Chapter 10

1. The longest and most detailed obituary for John Swaim appeared in the *Minutes of the Newark Conference of the Methodist Episcopal Church, 1876* , 52. A shorter version was published in the *Minutes of the General Conferences of the Methodist Episcopal Church*, 1876, 42; Samuel B. Darnell drafted yet another obituary for the *Christian Advocate*. For information about Mrs. Swaim, see "Catherine T. W. Swaim," *Minutes of the Newark Conference of the Methodist Episcopal Church, 1886* , 62; *Times-Union* (Jacksonville), March 2, 1886.

2. Quoted in Hedrick, *Harriet Beecher Stowe*, 396.

3. Ibid.

4. Ibid.

5. *New York Times*, August 27, 1886.

6. Ibid.

7. *New York Tribune*, August 27, 1886.

8. *New York Times*, August 27, 1886.

9. Perkins, "Two Years with a Colored Regiment," 533–43.

10. Charles Beecher, *Patmos*, 221.

11. Ibid.

12. Ibid.

13. Charles Beecher, *Spiritual Manifestations*, 93.

14. Charles Beecher, *Patmos*, 97.

15. Ibid., 95.

16. Harrison M. Reed, Jr., to Edward C. Williamson, March 15, 1953, Papers of the Florida Historical Society; Foster and Foster, "Chloe Merrick Reed," 297.

17. Harrison Reed to Senator John L. Mitchell, April 7, 1889, Mitchell Papers, State Historical Society of Wisconsin, Madison.

18. Reed to Mitchell, April 7, May 24, 1889.

19. MS, November 5, 1889; *Times-Union* (Jacksonville), July 4, 1890.

20. MS, December 11, 1889.

21. Ibid.

22. Ibid.

23. Quoted in MS, February 22, 1889.

24. Ibid.

25. *Florida Times-Union* (Jacksonville), September 1, 1890.

26. Harrison M. Reed, Jr., to Edward C. Williamson, March 15, 1953.

27. *Florida Times-Union* (Jacksonville), May 26, 1899.

28. Ibid.

29. Ibid.

30. Ibid.

31. Ibid.

32. Ibid.

33. Ibid.

34. Ibid.

35. Ibid.

36. Ibid.

Chapter 11

1. Foster, Whitmer, and Foster, "Tourism Was Not the Only Purpose," 318.

2. The ownership of the railroad is mentioned in Akin, *Flagler: Rockefeller Partner*, 134.

3. *New York Tribune*, February 17, 1877.

4. MS, November 5, 1889.

5. CU, May 8, 1872.

BIBLIOGRAPHY

Manuscripts and Collections

Beecher, Charles. Diary, March 5–20, 1867. Harriet Beecher Stowe Center (Stowe-Day Library), Hartford, Connecticut.
———. Florida Manuscripts. Harriet Beecher Stowe Center (Stowe-Day Library), Hartford, Connecticut.
———. Letters. American Missionary Association Papers, Amistad Research Center, Tulane University, New Orleans, Louisiana.
———. Letters. Special Collections, Bowdoin College Library, Brunswick, Maine.
Beecher Family Papers. Sterling Memorial Library, Yale University, New Haven, Connecticut.
Bureau of Refugees, Freedmen, and Abandoned Lands (BRFAL), Florida. Records, RG 105, National Archives, Washington, D.C.
Chase, Salmon. Papers. Library of Congress.
Merrick, Chloe. Letter. Gerrit Smith Papers, Syracuse University Library, Syracuse, New York.
Reed, Harrison. Mitchell Papers, State Historical Society of Wisconsin, Madison.
Reed, Harrison M., Jr. Papers of the Florida Historical Society, Melbourne, Florida.
Swaim, John. Diary, January 1, 1866–February 17, 1867. Private Collection of John and Sarah Foster, Tallahassee, Florida.
WPA Federal Writers' Project. "Interviews of Local Residents of Jacksonville (1936–1941)." Typescript, Jacksonville Public Library.

Newspapers and Periodicals

The American Freedman (New York), 1868–69.
Boston Daily Advertiser, 1868.
Boston Journal, 1863.
Christian Advocate and Journal (New York), 1865–66, 1872, 1876.
The Christian Union (New York), 1870, 1872–74, 1877.
Daily Standard (Syracuse), 1852, 1862–63, 1884.
Examiner (St. Augustine), 1869.
Florida Times-Union (Jacksonville), 1886, 1919.
Florida Union (Jacksonville), 1867, 1869, 1876.
Liberator (Boston), 1862–63.
Milwaukee Sentinel, 1869, 1889.
The National Freedman ((New York), 1865–66.
Newark Daily Advertiser, 1865.
New South (Jacksonville), 1874.
New York Times, 1886.
New York Tribune, 1865, 1877, 1886.
The Semi-Tropical (Jacksonville), 1875–78.
Sentinel of Freedom (Newark), 1865, 1867–68, 1875.
Syracuse Courier, 1875.
Syracuse Journal, 1856, 1863–66, 1869.
Tallahassee Sentinel, 1871–72.
True Wesleyan (New York), 1851.
Weekly Floridian (Tallahassee), 1873–74, 1876, 1880.

Other Published Sources

Akin, Edward N. *Flagler: Rockefeller Partner and Florida Baron.* Kent, Ohio: Kent State University Press, 1988.
Alvord, J. W. *Fourth Semi-Annual Report on Schools for Freedmen.* Washington, D.C.: United States Government Printing Office, 1867.
Anderson, Jervis. *A. Philip Randolph: A Biographical Portrait.* New York: Harcourt, Brace, Jovanovich, 1973.
Baldwin, A. S. "St. John's Bar." *Semi-Tropical* 2 (June 1876): 321–40.
Beecher, Charles. "A Century Hence." *Semi-Tropical* 4 (February 1878): 86–87.
———. "Florida a Hundred Years Hence." *Semi-Tropical* 3 (July 1877): 389–91.
———. *Patmos: Or, The Unveiling.* Boston: Lee and Sheppard, 1896.

———. "Report of the Superintendent of Public Instruction: For the Year Ending September 30, 1871." *Senate Journal,* 1873.

———. "Report of the Superintendent of Public Instruction: For the Year Ending September 30, 1872." *Senate Journal,* 1873.

———. *Spiritual Manifestations.* Boston: Lee and Sheppard, 1879.

———. "Supplementary Report to Governor O. B. Hart." *Senate Journal,* 1873.

Beecher, Eunice Bullard. *Letters from Florida.* New York: Appleton, 1879.

Brown, Canter, Jr. "Carpetbagger Intrigues, Black Leadership, and a Southern Loyalist Triumph: Florida's Gubernatorial Election of 1872." *Florida Historical Quarterly* 72 (January 1994): 275–301.

———. *Florida's Black Public Officials, 1867–1924.* Tuscaloosa, Alabama: University of Alabama Press, 1998.

———. *Florida's Peace River Frontier.* Orlando: University of Central Florida Press, 1991.

———. *Ossian Bingley Hart: Florida's Loyalist Reconstruction Governor.* Baton Rouge: Louisiana State University Press, 1997.

Bush, George Gary. *The History of Education in Florida.* Washington, D.C.: United States Government Printing Office, 1889.

Cash, William T. *The Story of Florida.* New York: American Historical Society, 1938.

"Catherine T. W. Swaim." *Minutes of the Newark Conference of the Methodist Episcopal Church, 1886.* New York, 1886.

Chandler, David Leon. *Henry Flagler: The Astonishing Life and Times of the Visionary Robber Baron Who Founded Florida.* New York: Macmillan, 1986.

Cochran, Thomas E. *History of Public School Education in Florida.* Tallahassee: State of Florida, 1921.

Covington, James W. *Plant's Palace: Henry B. Plant and the Tampa Bay Hotel.* Louisville: Harmony House, 1990.

Crooks, James B. *Jacksonville: After the Fire, 1901–1919.* Gainesville: University Presses of Florida, 1991.

Current, Richard N. *Those Terrible Carpetbaggers.* New York: Oxford University Press, 1988.

Daniels, Jonathan. *Prince of Carpetbaggers.* New York: J. B. Lippincott, 1958.

Davis, T. Frederick. *History of Jacksonville, Florida, and Vicinity, 1513 to 1924.* Gainesville: University of Florida Press, 1964.

Dovell, Junius E. *Florida: Historic, Dramatic, Contemporary.* New York: Lewis Historical Publishing Co., 1952.

Engs, Robert F. *Freedom's First Generation: Black Hampton, Virginia, 1861–1890.* Philadelphia: University of Pennsylvania Press, 1979.

Eppes, Susan Bradford. *Through Some Eventful Years*. Gainesville: University of Florida Press, 1968.

Foner, Eric. *Reconstruction: America's Unfinished Revolution, 1863 –1877* . New York: Harper and Row, 1988.

Foster, John T., Jr., and Sarah Whitmer Foster. "Aid Societies Were Not Alike: Northern Teachers in Post–Civil War Florida." *Florida Historical Quarterly* 72 (January 1995): 308–24.

———. "John Sanford Swaim: A Life at the Beginning of Modern Florida." *Methodist History* 26 (July 1988): 229–40.

———. "The Last Shall Be First: Northern Methodists in Reconstruction Jacksonville." *Florida Historical Quarterly* 70 (January 1992): 265–80.

———. "St. Augustine Visit in 1875." *Florida Living* (January 1988): 12–13.

Foster, John T., Jr., Herbert B. Whitmer, Jr., and Sarah Whitmer Foster. "Tourism Was Not the Only Purpose: Jacksonville Republicans and Newark's *Sentinel of Freedom*." *Florida Historical Quarterly* 63 (January 1985): 318–24.

Foster, Sarah Whitmer, and John T. Foster, Jr. "Chloe Merrick Reed: Freedom's First Lady." *Florida Historical Quarterly* 71 (January 1993): 279–99.

Futch, Ovid. "Salmon P. Chase and Civil War Politics in Florida." *Florida Historical Quarterly* 32 (April 1954): 163–88.

The General Conference of the Methodist Episcopal Church, 1792 to 1896 . Cincinnati: Curts and Jennings, 1900.

Graff, Mary B. *Mandarin on the St. Johns*. Gainesville: University of Florida Press, 1953.

Graham, Thomas. *The Awakening of St. Augustine: The Anderson Family and the Oldest City*. St. Augustine: St. Augustine Historical Society, 1978.

Gurko, Miriam. *The Ladies of Seneca Falls: The Birth of the Women's Rights Movement*. New York: Macmillan, 1974.

Harshorn, W. N. *An Era of Progress and Promise*. Boston: Priscilla, 1910.

Hedrick, Joan D. *Harriet Beecher Stowe: A Life*. New York: Oxford University Press, 1994.

Hull, Forrest P. *Georgetown: Story of One Hundred Years, 1838 –1938* . Georgetown, Mass.: Jones, 1938.

Johnson, Allen. *Dictionary of American Biography*. Vol. 2. New York: Charles Scribner's, 1929. Vol. 13. New York: Charles Scribner's, 1934.

Kingman, Peter D. *Neither Dies nor Surrenders: A History of the Republican Party in Florida*. Gainesville: University of Florida Press, 1984.

Lee, Luther. *Woman's Right to Preach the Gospel*. Syracuse, New York, 1853.

Minutes of the Newark Conference of the Methodist Episcopal Church, 1876 . New York, 1876.

Morrow, Ralph E. *Northern Methodism and Reconstruction.* East Lansing, Michigan: Michigan State University Press, 1956.

New Jersey Conference Memorial Containing Biographical Sketches of All Its Deceased Members. Philadelphia: Perkinpine and Higgins, 1865.

Perkins, Frances Beecher. "Two Years with a Colored Regiment: A Woman's Experience." *New England Magazine* 17 (January 1898): 533–43.

Proctor, Samuel. "The University of Florida: Its Early Years." Ph. D. diss., University of Florida, 1958.

Reed, Harrison. "Governor's Message to the Legislature." *Assembly Journal: A Journal of the Proceedings of the State of Florida.* Tallahassee: State of Florida Printer, 1871.

———. "Opinions of the Press." *Semi-Tropical* 1 (December 1875): 256–58.

———. "Our Magazine." *Semi-Tropical* 1 (October 1875): 128–29.

Rerick, Rowland H. *Memoirs of Florida.* Atlanta: Southern Historical Association, 1902.

Richardson, Joe M. "A Northerner Reports on Florida: 1866." *Florida Historical Quarterly* 40 (April 1962): 381–90.

Robinson, Solon. "A Lesson for Florida." *Semi-Tropical* 2 (February 1876): 79–81.

Rugoff, Milton. *The Beechers: An American Family in the Nineteenth Century.* New York: Harper and Row, 1981.

Schuckers, Jacob. W. *The Life and Public Services of Salmon Portland Chase: United States Senator and Governor of Ohio, Secretary of the Treasury and Chief Justice of the United States.* New York: D. Appleton, 1874.

Schwartz, Gerald. *A Woman Doctor's Civil War: Esther Hill Hawk's Diary.* Columbia: University of South Carolina Press, 1984.

Scott, J. Irving E. *The Education of Black People in Florida.* Philadelphia: Dorrance, 1974.

Sheats, William N. "Twenty-Fifth and Twenty-Sixth Annual Report of the Department of Public Instruction." *House Journal,* 1895.

Shofner, Jerrell H. *Nor Is It Over Yet: Florida in the Era of Reconstruction, 1863 – 1877.* Gainesville: University Florida Press, 1974.

Silliman, Justus M. *A New Canaan Private in the Civil War: The Letters of Justus M. Silliman.* New Canaan, Connecticut: New Canaan Historical Society, 1984.

Simpson, Brooks D., Leroy P. Graf, and John Muldown. *Advice after Appomattox.* Knoxville: University of Tennessee Press, 1987.

Stowe, Charles Edward. *Life of Harriet Beecher Stowe: Compiled from Her Letters and Journals.* New York: Houghton, Mifflin, 1890.

Stowe, Harriet Beecher. "Education of Freedmen." *North American Review* 128 (June 1879): 605–15.

———. "Education of Freedmen, Part II." *North American Review* 129 (July 1879): 81–95.

———. "Our Florida Plantation." *Atlantic Monthly* 43 (May 1879): 641–49.

———. *Palmetto-Leaves.* Boston: James R. Osgood, 1873.

———. "Protect the Birds." *Semi-Tropical* 3 (January 1877): 33–34.

———. *Uncle Tom's Cabin, or Life among the Lowly.* 1852. New York: Penguin Putnam, 1998.

———. "Villa Alexandria." *Semi-Tropical* 3 (August 1877): 448–51.

Stowe, Lyman Beecher. *Saints, Sinners, and Beechers: An American Family in the Nineteenth Century.* Indianapolis: Bobbs-Merrill, 1934.

Stowell, Jay S. *Methodist Adventures in Negro Education.* New York: Methodist Book Concern, 1922.

Ward, James R. *Old Hickory's Town.* Jacksonville: Florida Publishing Co., 1982.

Williams, Robert. "A Century of Compromise: On the Status and Role of Blacks in the Church and Society." Ph.D. diss., Drew University, 1983.

Williamson, Edward C. *Florida Politics in the Gilded Age, 1877–1893.* Gainesville: University of Florida Press, 1976.

Wood, Wayne W. *Jacksonville's Architectural Heritage.* Jacksonville: University of North Florida Press, 1989.

Index

Abolitionism, 5–6, 7, 8

Adams, J. S., 64–65

African Americans: agriculture and, 37, 39–40; Ansel Kinne on conditions of, 39–40; Charles Beecher on, 47; Chloe Merrick Reed on rights of, 36; creation of congregation of, 40–41; education of (*see* Education: of African Americans); freedmen's aid societies and, 8–9, 16–17; Harriet Beecher Stowe on, 92; Harrison Reed and, 64, 85; higher education for, 80–81; in Jacksonville, 56, 127; on reinstitution of slavery, 35–36; suffrage for, 17–18, 59; Swaim's immigration plan and, 29, 56; teachers' opinions of, 16

African Methodist Episcopal Church (AME), 61–62, 63, 81, 122

Agriculture: African Americans and, 37, 39–40; *Boston Daily Advertiser* on, 55–56; freezes and, 113; Harriet Beecher Stowe on, 44, 89–90; *Newark Sentinel of Freedom* on, 97–98; planters and, 37, 39–40; Swaim on, 42, 55

Aid societies, 8–9, 16–17, 33–34, 36. *See also* National Freedmen's Relief Association (NFRA)

Amelia Island, 9. *See also* Fernandina

Anders, Lymas, 40

Andersonville prisoners, 27–28, 30–31

Anthony, Susan B., 6

Armstrong, Samuel Chapman, 16

Atlantic Monthly, 109

Baldwin, A. S., 104

Baptists, 60, 62

Beecher, Charles, 34; on African Americans, 47; articles for *Semi-Tropical*, 104–6; assistance to Harriet Beecher Stowe, 3–4, 47; background of, 3–4, 52–53; on Bloxham, 86; description of Florida, 46, 48, 53, 54; educational reforms of, 77–80, 126; effect of Florida on, 110; family life of, 53, 137n.26; Henry Ward Beecher on, 137n.26; heresy trial of, 52; impeachment of Harrison Reed and, 66; leaving of Florida by, 118; Newport farm of, 96; portrait of, *following page 58* ; purchase of Newport land by, 54; on socialism and evolution, 118–19; as state superintendent of public instruction, 75–80

Beecher, Eunice Bullard, 110–11, 125–26

Beecher, Frankie, 22–25, 118

Beecher, Henry Ward, 25; adultery trial of, 117; on Charles Beecher, 137n.26; *Christian Union* of, 88; economic depression and, 93

Beecher, James Chapman, 21–25, 117–18, *portrait following page 58*

Beecher, Lyman, 52

Beecher, William Constantine, 70, 106

Berea College, 109

Bethune, Mary McCloud, 127

Bethune-Cookman College, 127

Billings, Liberty, 60, 62

Black codes, 33, 35